Effective Networking Skills

Your Master Guide to Building your Net Worth!

Gerard Assey

Effective Networking Skills

By

Gerard Assey

Published by:
Gerard Assey
19/18, Palli Arasan Street
Anna Nagar East
Chennai - 600 102

ISBN: 978-93-92492-36-5

Cover Image: Image by rawpixel.com on Freepik- Courtesy www.Freepik.com
Due acknowledgement is provided. Thank you.

Table of Contents

Introduction

"Networking is not just about connecting people. It's about connecting people with people, people with ideas, and people with opportunities that are mutually beneficial".

Networking is a major part of any career or business, whether you're seeking advancement opportunities, building a client base for your business, or expanding your business, this skill has long been identified as a key method to give you that one-up and competitive edge in the marketplace.

Networking skills are essential in both personal and professional environments, as building your professional network helps you connect with individuals who can help your business, or in a job search process or offer support to advance your career, or just help you with some new ideas and thoughts.

It is all about the process of establishing a mutually beneficial relationship with other like-minded professionals and potential clients and/or customers, by helping you with the sharing of knowledge, ideas and expertise and building your professional profile. For this reason, Networking can be looked at as just another name for the conversations and relationships you have with people in your personal and professional communities, while you are pursuing your professional goals.

Life requires us to effectively manage 4 Key components if we have to be successful... Think of the acronym **C.R.A.F.T:**

Change

Relationships
Attitude
Finances
Time

Anyone of these 5 components if not managed well, can lead to a disrupted life, and as we can see 'Relationships' is one of the essential keys

Relationship building skills are therefore crucial not just in building your business, especially when working on building your network, but life as a whole- as this can help create the foundation of care, trust and connection that we need to enable us grow. They enable you to get the best from others- partners and collaborators, and work towards your goals. A successful relationship is built on trust, respect and understanding, and requires ongoing investment from both parties.

Building good work relationships can take hard work. It requires time, patience, and self-awareness. But putting in the emotional labor and building good work relationships will help you feel more connected and increase your overall satisfaction and network, along with the net worth that comes along. In fact businesses are increasingly looking for candidates with strong relationship or networking skills. A company culture that encourages employees to maintain healthy relationships can go a long way towards enhancing employee well-being and building powerful networks.

But, sometimes, networking with strangers can seem a little daunting, nerve-wracking and sometimes downright awkward, and maybe for this reason, many people struggle to understand the importance of networks and often neglect to develop these skills for success in this area. But as you will see in the following pages of this highly practical guide: **'Effective Networking Skills'**- an effective tool that is often misunderstood- this powerful book would help you get your approach right to networking and off to a great start, or if you're an experienced networker, build on your existing skills immensely enabling you: recognize its importance in a professional development context; evaluate networking opportunities, know how to make networking a more natural exercise; develop confidence, and know how to apply these skills of effective networkers in building long lasting relationships.

So here's to a Great start in building your Net Worth!

What Exactly is Networking?
Why Network?
The Benefits of Networking

Let's start by answering this question: What is Networking?

Merriam-Webster Dictionary defines Networking as: "*The exchange of information or services among individuals, groups, or institutions; specifically, the cultivation of productive relationships for employment or business.*"

However, here is what I feel best defines it: *"The action of interacting with others to exchange information, ideas, resources and develop contacts, using the personal relationships people have with one another to further help increase exposure to information and opportunity- overall building two way relationships which could possibly lead to newer opportunities that are mutually beneficial. In fact it is more about giving and NOT just getting"*

Networking is an unfortunate term because it implies connections but ignores the importance of true relationships. Networking is in fact about connecting with people on a personal level. It's a quality-led relationship, not demanding or only about expecting benefits in return but a human-to-human endeavour where we can share commonality either in-person or online, ultimately resulting in opportunities for both sides that are beneficial

Why do we need to Network- What are the Benefits?

According to surveys, 75% - 80% of business is obtained as a direct result of some sort of networking. There is some truth in the old saying: *"It is not what you know, but who you know."* So Networking is the key to your business success

And if you look at the job market, 75%-90% of jobs are a part of the hidden job market that is accessible only by networking, with about 70% of all jobs found through networking (personal/professional contacts and research) and about 85% of people are hired as the result of networking or some other type of referral or personal contact.

A few years ago, LinkedIn conducted a study on the value of networking. The headline finding stated that '80% of professionals consider professional networking to be important to career success'

Remember, that every person you meet has 200-250 people with whom they connect, who can potentially assist you, and anyone that you might want to meet or contact in the world, is finally only 5 to 6 people contacts away from you

So here are a few main benefits of Networking?

- ✓ Access to knowledge through contacts
- ✓ Develop contacts that can provide with support, ideas and advice
- ✓ Learn from other people
- ✓ Create collaborations
- ✓ Can create otherwise unknown chances for collaboration, job openings and new opportunities.
- ✓ Development of your emotional and creative intelligence though added support and advice,

including the support from mentors and champions

- ✓ Exposure to new environments
- ✓ Helps build and increase self-confidence and social kills
- ✓ Enhances communication skills
- ✓ Improves elevator pitch
- ✓ Helps in finding mentors
- ✓ Stronger business connections
- ✓ Helps develop personal relationships
- ✓ Exposure to environments in which your career interests operate
- ✓ Helps find a job you love
- ✓ Helps interact with a group of like-minded people for collaboration and validation
- ✓ Is a way of learning about opportunities which may be hidden from you and can connect you with people who have such experiences
- ✓ Access to a wider pool of ideas through chances to discuss any research you are undertaking.
- ✓ Raises your own profile with new skill sets
- ✓ You are a valuable addition to other people's networks and they will benefit from the connection with you.

Barriers to Networking

At the very thought of the word 'networking', I know of many who feel very uncomfortable about approaching people, talking about themselves and asking people to connect with them.

As you will see, there are the several reasons or barriers that keep putting people off (for example, low self confidence, lack of focus, coming out of your comfort zone, lack of preparation etc), but, having an understanding of these barriers, and applying the new skills you are about to learn from this book, you will through practice, be able to overcome these barriers and move forward successfully, without any hindrances.

So what then are these blocks that can come in the way?

- ✓ Shyness
- ✓ Cultural differences – not knowing the rules of different societies/cultures and attitudes to small talk / direct questions / speaking to strangers
- ✓ Not comfortable with people you don't know- without a frame of reference, how to start a conversation?
- ✓ The awkwardness of starting conversations
- ✓ Not knowing what to say
- ✓ Feeling intimidated by people who know more than you/ higher in positions
- ✓ Talking to people with more status
- ✓ Fear of embarrassment: Because you likely respect someone, that respect that you have can lead to fear that can embarrass you
- ✓ Saying something stupid/ irrelevant

- ✓ Insecurity
- ✓ Herd mentality: When people are grouped together it can influence how they behave and that may keep you from joining into the conversation
- ✓ Pressurized and a feeling that I have to network
- ✓ Not knowing where to meet the right people

Key Attributes and Traits of Great Networkers

Networking involves interacting with others and being cognizant of other people's expectations while adjusting our behaviour accordingly if we want to make a positive impression that will help build a powerful network.

In many surveys carried out, following were found to be some of the key traits or attributes of highly successful networkers. Using the list below, you could work to develop the ones you do not possess or are weak in:

- ✓ Positive Attitude: The first thing that people see from you is your attitude, how you perceive things in general. A consistently negative attitude makes people move away from you and will thus drive away referrals; On the other hand positive professionals are like magnets, with others wanting to be around you- directing others to you.
- ✓ High Self-Esteem: You know who you are. You value and respect yourself and others. You know you strengths and areas that you need to improve on. This gives you the confidence to carry yourself high- but not arrogance!
- ✓ Approachable: People *"will forget what you said and what you did, but they will never forget how you made them feel."* Effective networking starts with approachability. How comfortable did you make the other person
- ✓ Presentable: Your appearance and grooming: You never get a second chance to make a first

impression. How well you maintain your personal hygiene and how well you dress for the occasion speaks volumes without saying one word. You don't want to be the one that feels out of place.

- ✓ Authenticity and Sincerity: You can smell authenticity from a mile away- the feeling you get when you speak with them. Authenticity and sincerity are transparent. You can act interested, but even if you are not; it will be reflected in your mannerisms, which can really put people off. You know that if they give their word, they will keep it no matter what.
- ✓ Collaborative/ Helping Others: People don't care how much you know until they know how much you care, and helping people shows that you really care. Helping others can be done in a variety of ways, from sending a clip of a helpful article or to by putting them in touch with a person who can help them with a specific challenge.
- ✓ Active Listener: If you let people talk and share their stories, experiences and opinions, they will remember they had a great experience with you. The best networkers are the ones who actively listen to the other person. Listening is an active process in which a conscious decision is made to listen to and understand the messages of the speaker. Active listening is also about patience, by not interrupting with questions or comments and giving the other person time to explore their thoughts and feelings
- ✓ Good Communicator: At networking events, you may interact with a large group of people

to build connections, requiring excellent public speaking skills that will help the other person understand what you are trying to say.

- ✓ A Positive Approach: It is important to understand that behaviour is a form of communication, so be mindful of your body language. It can say a lot about you. Work on things such as your posture and your tone of voice when engaged in communication.
- ✓ Trustworthy: Trust is vital in any relationship. Never share confidential information you hear through others unless you have permission to do so. Always keep the promises you make to others in your network; set realistic expectations and be sure to meet them.
- ✓ Empathy: People prefer sharing their emotions and experience with empathetic people-people that feel and care. Asking questions related to the situation and approaching a situation based on the viewpoint of others can help you network better with people.
- ✓ Proactive: Simply waiting for people to contact you will only give you a fraction of the benefits that reaching out to new or existing contacts can offer. Set for yourself a stretching, but achievable target that can be helpful of making sure you remain proactive. Think and plan ahead
- ✓ Knowledgeable: Need to be updated on current events/ activities/ happenings in your industry/ field/ circle
- ✓ Being Thick skinned: Get comfortable hearing the word “no”, over and over and over again. It will build your character and make you tenacious about your business and career.

- ✓ More Givers than Takers: Even when you do not share an interest with someone, you can probably find something valuable to offer by thinking beyond the obvious. An off course, this isn't always easy.

Why Self-Esteem Matters for a Networker How to Build a High Self-Esteem!

Self-esteem refers to a person's beliefs about their own worth and value. It also has to do with the feelings people experience that follows from their sense of worthiness or unworthiness. Self-esteem is important because it heavily influences people's choices and decisions.

People with high self-esteem are also people who are motivated to take care of themselves and to persistently strive towards the fulfilment of personal goals and aspirations. People with lower self-esteem don't tend to regard themselves as worthy of happy outcomes or capable of achieving them and so tend to let important things slide and to be less persistent and resilient in terms of overcoming adversity.

So it is important to appreciate how low self-esteem can have a major impact on your networking efforts if it is not at least basically understood and addressed.

An individual with high self-esteem is likely to build their network by having a positive, open and 'can do' attitude. Conversely, an individual with low self-esteem is likely to lack that belief in him/ herself to start with. They will convince themselves (and others) that they have little that would be of interest to others in any network.

Confidence versus Self-Esteem

A lot has been said and published with a great debate on the subject of 'Confidence'. A lot of Sales people want to be more confident, without knowing the actual meaning of it.

A few points to note about confidence is that; it is 'External' and it is 'Temporary'. When I say external- I mean that in most times it is <u>not</u> in your Control- somebody else is most of the time controlling it. When I say it is temporary I believe that for a day our confidence levels fluctuate several times depending on situations, circumstances, the people and environment we are in. That is why we do not recommend that Sales People aim at only Confidence.

Here is an example of what I mean:

You come into the office in the morning in a good mood-upbeat and all excited with a set of appointments you have for the day. However, your boss calls you into his cabin and pulls you up for a complaint that has come in from a top customer. What happens to your confidence level...One that was upbeat, is now down depending on how hard he came upon you!

Later, that same evening, you have bagged a huge order from another customer and that same boss now praises you as one of his best performers. What happens now? You are on top of the world, all up beat and charged up again.

As you can see in a single day your confidence levels can vary and fluctuate, which means they are temporary. Most times it is the effect or impact of others that have changed that feeling. It is like someone having a remote control on your life and your moods that can change or impact it every now and then.

A better, permanent solution to this is for you as a Professional is to work on having a High Self Esteem. First let us look at what is Self Esteem?

Simply put...It is how much you value or respect yourself! The more you value or respect yourself, then, when you do face such situations like the example we've just seen, you are able to stay above- your value if it is 100, stays 100 and does not change! You now know that your boss has pulled you up for something wrong that you had done- but that does not change your value- it still remains 100.

Building your Self Esteem

Say out loud:

"I am the Most Valuable Person at work".

"I am the Most Valuable Person at my work". (Repeat it)

It's true. You are the most valuable person. No one else can quite fill your shoes. No one else can be you. You bring your unique being to work every day. You bring with you your talents, your abilities, your knowledge, your skills, your personality, or just your plain know-how. You may not be using all of your abilities just yet. You may not be using them to the fullest. You may not even recognize how valuable a person you are.

Healthy Self Esteem, not narcissistic, self-indulgent, or arrogance means to appreciate the value of you as a unique human being with your own special talents and abilities.

The word "esteem" in Latin, means, *"to value highly"*

It would be impossible to value another person without first feeling valuable for yourself. When you place value on your own work and efforts, you can begin to find value in the work of others.

The Self-Image: Highway to Success

Have you ever said to yourself the following?

'I can't imagine myself being successful'

'I would like to, but I don't have enough experience or the right education'

'I can't get ahead because I'm too short, overweight, not good looking, my parents are poor, etc'.

The truth is most people talk themselves into failure and dejection. The result is the Fear of Trying.

Most of us know of or have read about common, everyday people who have become uncommonly productive and successful in their work and careers; individuals who have overcome enormous outer obstacles and inner roadblocks to become great.

Yet many people can't imagine doing such things themselves. They say, "*Yes, he could do it or she's doing it, but I can't because of_______________".*

They develop the habit of failure. And it takes two forms:

Failure Reinforcement-the habit of looking back at past problems

Failure Forecasting-the habit of imagining the worst in the future

Because they lack sufficient self-esteem to believe in the validity of their dreams, they don't prepare for their achievement, and therefore are going down a dead-end street.

No wonder so many people feel trapped. Failure becomes set in their self-images.

Never put yourself down- the workplace is full of put-downs- Don't do it yourself!

Self Esteem Takes Practice

Believe in yourself, no matter how long it takes or how tough it may seem at times.

There was once a college professor whose wife had a hearing deficiency. In trying to invent a device to enhance her hearing, he created something more complex that he thought might be useful to the public. He traveled throughout the New England states trying to find venture capital to take his idea into production. But businessmen everywhere laughed at him. *"Ideas are a dime a dozen."* They said: *"The project is doomed to failure."* Thank goodness, Alexander Graham Bell had the self-esteem to hang in there even when his only reward was his belief in himself.

Often we put imaginary barriers in our paths when no such barriers actually exist. In the 1940s, the greatest physicist and aeronautical engineers believed that the sound barriers could not be broken-that everyone or anything would be shattered when it approached the speed of sound. One lone pilot, Chuck Yeager, didn't believe it. He didn't think there was such a thing as sound "barrier". And indeed, he flew right through it.

Your Formula for Building a High Self-Esteem

How much you like yourself is the core energy force that determines your personality.

All STAR Performers have a program or formula for building self-esteem.

Steps You Can Take To Feel Better:

1. Action precedes feeling. Act your way into feeling something. Action triggers emotion. The role of pretending- act happy!
2. Set clear goals, so you can feel like a winner. Establish a VICTORY LIST for all your accomplishments. Set income goals (the WHAT) and personal goals (the WHY)
3. Accept 100% responsibility. "IF IT'S TO BE, IT'S UP TO ME." Or "IF IT'S ALL FOR ME, IT'S UP TO ME". No excuses, no blaming.

4. Commit yourself to excellence. LEARN TO BE THE BEST in whatever you do. Say to yourself: *'I'M THE BEST (and) I LOVE MY WORK'*

5. Mental Rehearsal: Visualize the outcomes you desire, especially before you go to sleep at night. See yourself as strong, confident and relaxed, and see your customers responding positively.

6. Get yourself a small note pad. Every night write down at least 3 positive things you did for that day- (it could be as small as even helping a person cross the road). Forget the negatives. Most times we go to bed filling our minds with all the negatives that occurred during the day. Just reverse it now. Look at only the positives. At the end of the year, you would have over one thousand positive things about you. Do you need any else then to tell you?

7. Believe in yourself-FAITH! Believe in yourself, your company and your products.

8. INTEGRITY AND HONESTY. They are at the root of success in sales. Never expect to be successful without being willing to pay the price. Never expect the rewards without working. Don't look for shortcuts.

9. Have confident expectations. Look for the good in every situation. Expect the best.

10. Practice the Law of Increasing Returns-the more your give thanks, the more you will have thanks for.

Managing You-Positive First Impressions!
It Begins by Selling Yourself First!

Have you ever wondered about the impressions you could create even before you open our mouth?
In a study carried out that I am about to share with you now, you will notice that people place more emphasis on what they SEE rather than on what they HEAR. So this only tells us that we need to be very careful with our body language and what we are projecting.
According to studies carried out, Communication takes place in 3 forms:

- ✓ Your Words
- ✓ Your Tone and
- ✓ Your Body Language.

Where 55% has to do with your Body Language or what others 'See'
7 % has to do with 'What' you say or your words
Whilst 38% has to do with 'How' those words are said, which is your Tone or voice modulation
With people going by what they SEE first rather than what they HEAR, it makes it very important for us to therefore project the RIGHT image upfront. That's the first impression that has been formed-good or bad! If it is good, then very good for you, but if it is bad, then so sad! Because…now you have double work to undo the wrong impression that has already gone into the mind and to now fill it with the right impression.
They say 90% of lasting impressions are created in the first 90 seconds. That can be really dangerous,

but surprisingly that is true! So we have to be very careful, with what are we projecting as soon as someone sees us, because that's what they will remember.

It is also a reason why we tend to remember a song seen on a television set better than when heard through a radio. The same logic applies at a job interview with your resume and the presentation of it! Then at the interview-the interviewer has made up his mind to a great extent as you walk in, even before you have opened your mouth. Your bio-profile or the interview process is only a confirmation of the decision already made in the mind of the interviewer.

Why is Tone next important after Body Language? Simply because you can say a same sentence with a different tone and that can change the entire meaning

Eg; "Mary come here" is a simple sentence. But depending on the right tone, this one sentence could turn out as an 'order 'or a 'request'.

Another stronger example: "Hang him not let him go"...could be death or life depending on how it is said. Example: 'Hang him, not let him go'! Or 'Hang him not, let him go'!

Now, if it is face to face, we may be able to save the situation, but when on the phone with the other person not able to see you, it could lead to miscommunication if the right tone is not used.

As seen earlier, with people going by what they 'See' first rather than what they 'Hear', it makes it so very important for us to therefore project the RIGHT image upfront. It basically involves Selling Yourself first!

Before a customer buys anything or decides to do business with you or the company that you represent, he needs to first be sold on you because you are what he sees about your company to him. Your company could have a several floor building, with several offices all across the globe. But to the person doing business with you, what he sees in you is the impression he has formed of your company! Because…90% of lasting impressions are created in the first 90 seconds

A person forms an impression of you, usually in less than ten seconds, based on a combination of some of these attributes:

- ✓ Posture, Walk
- ✓ Body language
- ✓ Attire, Clothing
- ✓ Physical characteristics
- ✓ Smile, Facial features
- ✓ Handshake
- ✓ Cleanliness, Grooming
- ✓ Scent, perfume
- ✓ Eye contact
- ✓ Perceived Confidence

In a study, men and women were asked to list the attributes they found attractive and unattractive in someone they met. And here is the list of some of the top responses:

Qualities that create a Positive Impression:

- ✓ Warmth
- ✓ Sense of humor
- ✓ Imagination
- ✓ Fitness
- ✓ Individuality
- ✓ Positive body language
- ✓ Conversational ability
- ✓ Creativity
- ✓ Kindness

Qualities that create a Negative Impression

- ✓ Self-centered
- ✓ Closed minded
- ✓ Judgmental
- ✓ Lack of manners
- ✓ Poor conversational ability
- ✓ Negative attitude
- ✓ Indecisiveness
- ✓ Lack of integrity
- ✓ Complaining and whining
- ✓ Politics and Power games
- ✓ Manipulation

Making a Great First Impression

If you want to make a good impression, know that you need to project **3 C's:**

Confidence

- ✓ Have a straight but relaxed posture. Hold your head high and steady. Don't slouch or slump.
- ✓ Move in a natural, unaffected manner.
- ✓ Maintain eye contact with the people you are talking to.

Competence

- ✓ Exhibit your knowledge when required. Know your way around the agenda. Be prepared for the meeting. Bring supportive materials to emphasize your points.
- ✓ Answer questions in a clear and professional manner, avoiding the use of slang or technical jargon.
- ✓ Ask relevant questions if needed.

Credibility

- ✓ Arrive on time.
- ✓ Be presentable (well-groomed and mindful of dress codes)

- ✓ Keep true to your word.
- ✓ When uncertain, err on the side of what you presume is conservatism. And be observant; check if people are becoming uncomfortable.
- ✓ Etiquette mishaps can range from merely embarrassing to potentially insulting to the other person. When you realize that you have committed a faux pas, apologize immediately and ask how you can make up for it

Appearance IS Everything! It starts with your Personal Grooming

Paying attention to your grooming by taking care of your cleanliness and your clothing demonstrates respect for yourself and for others- the key words being neat and clean.

- ✓ A general rule of thumb is: the more expensive the products/services you sell, the more professional you should look-Customers make assumptions about you based on your appearance.
- ✓ If it's an expensive product you are selling, the customer is bound to think: "How can this person help us make this expensive purchase when he can't even afford a proper wardrobe and take care of himself?"

Projecting the Right Image!

- ✓ How you dress, how you groom yourself and how you handle yourself in public is all part of your "packaging"
- ✓ Like product packaging, you can present yourself to be most appealing. And, you can present yourself differently according to the time and place.

- ✓ Presence is how you “present” yourself- it’s your self-confidence, poise and appeal.

So what does it take to make a Special, Positive, and Instant Impression when prospective ‘buyers’ first see you.

According to Drew Westen, in his fabulous book "The Political Brain" one of the main determinants of electoral success," he explains, "is simply a candidate's curb appeal”. Curb appeal is the feeling voters get when they 'drive by' a candidate a few times on television and form an emotional impression! Personal Curb Appeal is primarily a nonverbal process.

How's your Personal Curb Appeal? When your co-workers, clients, and business partners "drive by" you, how do you come across? Here are a few tips to keep in mind:

- ✓ Dress for success: Always dress and see yourself for the next level!
- ✓ Your motto should be: "Wear great clothes. You never know whom you'll meet!" When it comes to curb appeal, the way you dress matters. Clothing has an effect on both the observer and the wearer.
- ✓ Dressing for success doesn't necessarily mean you have to wear a suit to work. Many organizations have a more casual dress code. But it does mean that whatever you wear should help you make the statement that you are a competent professional.

The finest clothing made is a person's skin, but, of course, society demands something more than this- Mark Twain

Wardrobe Management

Your dress is either working for you or against you. Clothes send a message about how you want others to see you. The way you dress can play a big role in your professional career. Part of the culture of a company is the dress code of its employees. Some companies prefer a business casual approach, while other companies require a business professional dress code.

These guidelines provided, are only suggestions, as you would need to always research the event, function, occasion or environment in question to determine the appropriate dress attire. Each industry-professional, community, and academic, may sometimes follow its own wardrobe standards and traditions.

But remember: If you are not too sure when business casual is appropriate, then always remember the general rule of thumb: *It's better to be over-dressed, than under-dressed.*

Professional Dressing:

Business attire suggests formal, conservative dress style. Attention to detail, impeccable grooming, and a well-fitting suit are vital to make a good lasting impression.

The Suit: Choose a classic, neutral suit in charcoal, black, grey or navy. Avoid suits that conform to trends. Best fabrics for suits are wool/wool blends which can be worn all year and do not wrinkle easily. Skirt suits are appropriate feminine attire as long as the skirt hits or covers the knee and there are no large slits at the side, front, or back. The pant leg should touch the front of the shoe and fall just above the heel in the back. Make sure the suit flatters your body type and fits well, not too tight or loose.

The Dress Shirt: Choose shirts in a pale, subtle color (i.e., blue, cream, white, baby pink). Long sleeved, button-up shirts are most appropriate. Your shirt sleeve should extend beyond the suit jacket sleeves by half an inch. Pointed collars give a more professional image than button-down collars, yet both are acceptable. Choose shirts with more cotton than polyester; they resist wrinkling.

Shoes/Socks/Belt/Accessories etc:

Shoes: Leather in lace-ups shoes and should not be lighter than the trouser color. Shoes that match your suit or are slightly darker are the best choice in colors, such as brown, black, tan, or navy. The shoe should have a real sole (no sneakers, sandals, or street shoes) and a closed toe. Avoid platforms and heels higher than 2 inches. Shoes should be polished and in good condition. Wear black shoes with grey, navy or black suits and dark brown shoes with tan, brown or beige suits.

Socks: Preferable 100% cotton in black, brown, grey or navy. Choose a color to match or blend with trousers. Be sure to wear socks that cover your calves.

Ties: Tie and suit color should complement each other, but not match. Burgundy, red and navy blue work as good background colors. Small geometric prints and stripes are good choices. Paisleys with subdued patterns are alternatives. Silk ties are the preferred choice. They are elegant and can be worn all year in any climate. The tie knot should fill the space at the top of the shirt. Do not wear a matching handkerchief/ pocket square.

Belts: Either leather or reptile in black, brown or burgundy. Use discreet brass or good metal buckles. Suspenders are acceptable. Belts should be in good condition and match the color of your shoes, avoiding fancy and flashy buckles.

Briefcases: Briefcase should ideally be brown, black or burgundy leather, matching your shoes

Accessories: Jewellery ideally should be no more than one ring per hand. Good quality watches. No earring or studs for men

The right business attire never includes the following:

- ✓ Jeans (of any color)
- ✓ Athletic wear (e.g. sweat suits)
- ✓ Leggings
- ✓ T-shirts
- ✓ Low-cut garments, front or back
- ✓ Any kind of workout clothes, running or gym shoes, sneakers or sandals
- ✓ Hats, caps
- ✓ Ripped or tattered clothing
- ✓ Extremely tight-fitting clothes

What to keep in mind when buying your garments?

Before making a purchase, men and women need to answer "yes" to these key questions. If you are in doubt, don't buy the item, as clothes should look and feel good.

- ✓ Did you try the garment on?
- ✓ Did you check the fit in the front and the back?
- ✓ Is the suit jacket long enough to cover the buttocks?
- ✓ Are the button holes sewn tightly?
- ✓ Can you move around freely in the garment?
- ✓ Does the product feel comfortable?
- ✓ Check for pulls, bulges or bunching of the material.

- ✓ Do you like the garment? Buy a garment because you like it, not just to add to your wardrobe

How to Wear a Blazer or Suit

When planning to wear a blazer or a suit, here are a few tips on using them the right way. The first thing that you might want to consider when wearing a men's suit is how many buttons it will have. Although this may seem insignificant, the truth is that it is very important.

- ✓ When you wear a 3-button suit, you will button the top or top two buttons.
- ✓ When you wear a 2-button suit, you will button only the top button.
- ✓ With a 4-button suit, it is typically acceptable to button the two middle buttons, leaving the top button and the bottom button undone
- ✓ With a double-breasted suit, all buttons are buttoned.

When wearing a suit or Blazer:

- ✓ If you are seated, your suit coat should always be open. It is not acceptable to take off your suit coat unless you are to be seated for an extended period of time, like for a meal, or in your office, or if your host does so, etc.
- ✓ If you wish to take your suit coat off in company, it is polite to ask permission (Eg; - Do you mind if I take my coat off?)
- ✓ You should always hang your suit coat, even if only over the back of your chair

Wearing a Necktie- Combinations, Knots and Care

A tie is a man's way to express his personality and style.

Before you put on your tie:

- ✓ Check to make sure that the tie is clean, without any stains, grease or food spots
- ✓ Cut any loose threads on your tie. Pulling them can do damage to your tie.
- ✓ When wearing a shirt, tie and jacket, stick to a maximum of two different patterns unless you have a very solid fashion sense and know how to mix and match clothing well. Your tie should ideally be darker than the color of your shirt
- ✓ Always tie the knot in front of a mirror.
- ✓ Ensure your shirt is buttoned up, with a tie collar and have the collar up before putting the tie around your neck.
- ✓ Keep the knot of the tie tight throughout the entire tying process.
- ✓ The front of your tie should be just long enough so that the tip touches the waist of your pants.
- ✓ The general width of a tie that will not get out of style of fashion is 3.5 inches.
- ✓ Ideally, the width of a tie should match the width of the jacket's lapel. If the jacket has a wide lapel, then the tie should be wide, and if narrow, then the tie is narrow.
- ✓ So also, the knot of the tie should be proportional to the collar. It should not be so big that it spreads the collar of the shirt or forces it open, or so small that it gets lost in the collar of the shirt.

Caring for your Ties:

- ✓ A tie that is properly cared for can last forever.
- ✓ Untie your tie completely and hang up your ties. It helps take out some of the wrinkles and prevents damage.

- ✓ Knit ties can be stretched when hung, so gently roll them up and store them in a drawer.
- ✓ Ideally, ties must be hung on a rack designed for ties. Ties slip and twist on hangers and will probably fall off.
- ✓ When travelling, loosely roll ties and place them inside a pair of socks or use a tie case or box.
- ✓ Don't wear the same tie twice in a row. Ties need time to return to their normal shape

Necktie Knots

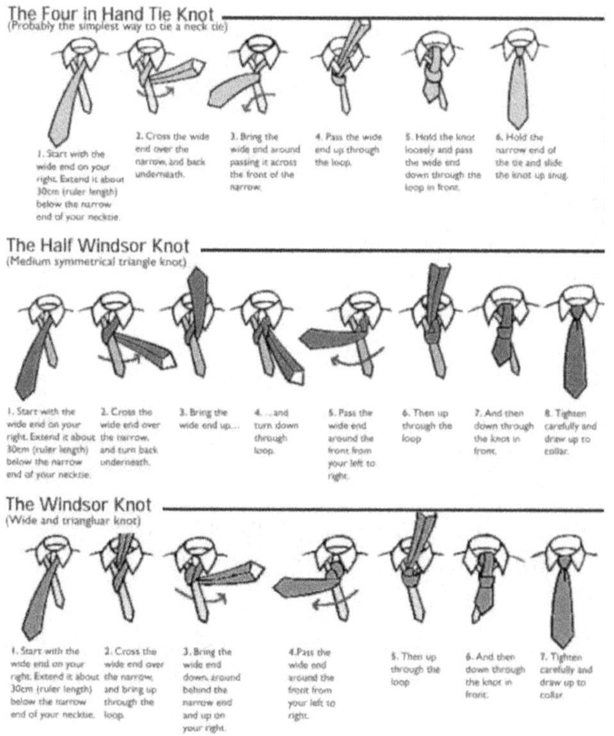

How to Tie Necktie Knots

The Four in Hand Tie Knot (Probably the simplest way to tie a neck tie)

1. Start with the wide end on your right. Extend it about 30cm (ruler length) below the narrow end of your necktie
2. Cross the wide end over the narrow, and back underneath
3. Bring the wide end around passing it across the front of the narrow
4. Pass the wide end up through the loop
5. Hold the knot loosely and pass the wide end down through the loop in front.
6. Hold the narrow end of the tie and slide the knot up snug.

The Half Windsor Knot (Medium symmetrical triangle knot

1. Start with the wide end on your right. Extend it about 30cm (ruler length) below the narrow end of your necktie.
2. Cross the wide end over the narrow, and turn back underneath.
3. Bring the wide end up....
4. And turn down through loop.
5. Pass the wide end around the front from your left to right.
6. Then up through the loop
7. And then down through the knot in front
8. Tighten carefully and draw up to collar.

The Windsor Knot (Wide and triangular knot)

1. Start with the wide end on your right. Extend it about 30cm (ruler length) below the narrow end of your necktie.
2. Cross the wide end over the narrow, and bring up through the loop

3. Bring the wide end down, around behind the narrow end and up on your right
4. Pass the wide end around the front from your left to right
5. Then up through the loop
6. And then down through the knot in front.
7. Tighten carefully and draw up to collar

The Meaning of Colors in Business that can help:
The colors you wear in professional settings and interviews can affect your mood, energy, and how others may perceive you. So you would want to wear colors that portray positive perceptions and exude confidence, sincerity, and reliability.
Here are some colors with their perceived meanings:

- ✓ Red: Action, powerful, passion and energetic
- ✓ Green: Growth, ideas, vitality and sophistication
- ✓ Blue: Inspires confidence, success and trust. Navy blue is best color for work/interviews – more likely to help create a positive vibe.
- ✓ Gold: Wealth, prosperity, luxury
- ✓ Black: Black looks classic and sophisticated, but perceived as depressing, serious or intimidating – so add a little color to black suits.
- ✓ Pink: Compassion, understanding and warmth. Pink or salmon worn by men is seen as a communicator color.
- ✓ Brown: Practical and reliable; sometimes perceived as dull
- ✓ Purple: Inventive, creative, intuitive. Dark purple can be perceived as elegant and projects authority.
- ✓ White: Clean, pure, innocent, and simple

Grooming Checklist

What could you do to improve your image- starting right from the top of your head to the tip of your toes- your hygiene, dressing and grooming, being organized etc.

Given below is a suggested checklist to help you project the Right Image!

Physical Aspects like:

- ✓ Personal Grooming-Dress for the next level!
- ✓ Cleanliness, Breath (floss/ use mouthwash), Hair well groomed, Nails, Body Odor (light deodorant)
- ✓ Clean, Wrinkle-free and Well-Pressed/ Proper fit clothes
- ✓ Check for stains/ lint/ holes/ loose buttons
- ✓ Pleasant Colors of Clothing
- ✓ Polished shoes and in good condition (don't let heels run down)
- ✓ Socks (clean without holes, foot deodorant?)
- ✓ Clean Spectacles
- ✓ Briefcase/ handbag well polished/ in good condition
- ✓ Business Cards in pristine, crisp condition (in a holder)
- ✓ Good quality pens that write!
- ✓ Standing- shoulder square/ sitting- erect
- ✓ Good Leather Bag/ Briefcase-organized /in order/ tidy

You might like to develop your own checklist now to suit your specific country and need.

(You might like to add on to the list above)

Your Body Language-What are you Conveying?

As we've seen, people form 90% of their opinion of us in the first 90 seconds, a good example of just how powerful first impressions are! Being dressed for success is good but not enough in the competitive times in which we live. How many people do you know that impress us with their clothes but fail to impress us in other ways? Body language is the way you stand, sit, the way you move, and the way you present yourself. A major percentage of what we communicate has nothing to do with words.

We communicate in a lot of other ways-by the way we sit, stand, tense our facial muscles, tap our fingers, shuffle our feet and uncross or cross our legs. Without saying a word, our body language is broadcasting so many things about us!

So here are some quick tips on what to do and not do!

How to Look Interested

- ✓ Make strong eye contact
- ✓ Tilt your head slightly
- ✓ Don't fidget
- ✓ Look upward
- ✓ Lean forward slightly, weight on balls of feet.

When someone is friendly, we also think of him as trustworthy, sincere and reliable.

How to Stand the Right Way

- ✓ Stand squarely in front of the person to whom you are speaking.
- ✓ It might sound strange, but you expose your heart and body.
- ✓ Don't turn sideways.
- ✓ Meet their eyes in a friendly but steady gaze.
- ✓ Smile in a warm, relaxed way

- ✓ Don't hold a book or purse in front of you or cross your arms.
- ✓ Use open hand gestures.

Maintaining the Right Physical Distance

- ✓ If you watch a crowd, you will notice that people stand at different distances from each other.
- ✓ Less than 18 inches: intimate
- ✓ 18 inches- 2.5 feet: close friends in a social gathering. You can hold out your arm and you can stick your thumb in the other person's ear! Try it!
- ✓ 2.5-4 feet: most people in a casual setting
- ✓ 4-12 feet: strangers
- ✓ 12 feet: a group of strangers
- ✓ If you get too close, the other person will grow tense or withdraw

Making Eye Contact

- ✓ The eyes have it. Well, they truly do, and can project confidence when there are no words.
- ✓ To be a good listener, let your eyes convey: "I'm listening"

Here are some Signs that can indicate Nervousness. Try to work on controlling these:

- ✓ Eyes darting back and forth
- ✓ Tensing of the body
- ✓ Contraction of the body
- ✓ Shifting one's weight from side to side
- ✓ Rocking in chair
- ✓ Crossing and uncrossing the arms or legs
- ✓ Tapping hands, fingers, or feet
- ✓ Adjusting or fiddling with pens, cups, eyeglasses, jewelry, clothing, fingernails, hair, or hands wringing hands
- ✓ Clearing the throat

- ✓ Coughing nervously
- ✓ Smiling nervously
- ✓ Biting the lip
- ✓ Looking down
- ✓ Chewing nails or picking cuticles
- ✓ Putting hands in pockets

And here are some Signs that can indicate Boredom. Try and work on controlling these too:

- ✓ Moving your body frequently
- ✓ Letting your eyes wander
- ✓ Gazing into the distance
- ✓ Glancing often at your watch
- ✓ Yawning
- ✓ Tapping fingers or feet
- ✓ Fidgeting
- ✓ Picking your fingers or nails
- ✓ Avoiding eye contact

Sitting, Standing and Walking the Right Way

The Right Way to Sit- for a Lady: If you are in someone's home or at a big social event, never sit, till you are given permission to do so. The hostess may have planned on a particular place she would like you to sit. If no one offers you, then only take the seat of your choice. Walk towards the chair with good posture. Turn and feel the chair with the back of your knees, just to make sure that no one has "accidentally" moved the chair away. Sit down, keeping your back straight and your head up, while keeping your knees together and you hands in your lap. Cross your legs at the ankle or hold your feet together. In any event, make sure your knees are together

The Right Way to Sit- for a Gentleman: Walk to the chair with good posture, and as you approach the chair, unbutton your jacket. Sit tall with your back against the chair and knees slightly apart and both feet on the floor, with your hands resting just above your knees. When you stand up, remember to re-button your jacket

Standing: When you get up, keep your feet parallel but your knees relaxed. Ensure that your spine is long and straight, with your shoulders back, stomach in, chest high, chin turned up slightly and your arms and hands relaxed.

Walking: Stand as mentioned above and step with feet slightly ahead of your body. This promotes good posture

Other Points: Never lean on anything, as it denotes a careless attitude with 99% of your "presence" being lost when you lean.

Never greet someone with a handshake across the table (the only exception of course is when you're meeting someone and both of you are seated).

Always stand up when you are shaking hands. Greeting someone from behind a desk creates an instant barrier. Instead, always greet someone as your equal

Meeting and Greeting

Greeting someone you know is a vital part of courtesy and goodwill. All societies and cultures have some form of greeting that is basic to civilized interaction. The first point about greetings is to *do them*. It's important to say "hello" even when you feel a bit off or shy. It's also important to make introductions even when you're not certain of precisely how it should be done in that situation. Every greeting and introduction is an opportunity to demonstrate respect for others and to create a favorable impression of you to others.

Your goal therefore within the first few minutes of meeting and greeting other people is to make them feel comfortable and to put them at ease so they will want to do business with you. Doing so will make the first encounter and subsequent ones go smoothly and easily. Getting off on the wrong foot can cause a difficult recovery

So let's first start with the most important thing you could do when meeting someone that doesn't cost you anything, before we get into the etiquette of handshaking and business cards and the other areas: And that's your Smile!

Your Smile will take you a Mile! It's been said many times- smile when someone enters your office and do it with feeling. Nothing makes a client feel more welcomed than a warm and friendly smile. Check yourself in a mirror to see yourself as the customer might see you…SMILE!

A smile is an invitation, a sign of welcome. It says, "I'm friendly and approachable."

The human brain prefers happy faces, recognizing them more quickly than those with negative expressions. In fact, a smile is such an important signal to social interaction, that it can be recognized from 300 feet- more than a football field away.

Most importantly, smiling directly influences how other people respond to you. When you smile at someone, they almost always smile in return. And, because facial expressions trigger corresponding feelings, the smile you get back changes people's emotional state in a positive way. This one simple act will instantly and powerfully increase your curb appeal.

On the phone-Your customer will not hear it, but will see and feel it! It's such an important aspect that can say a lot about you! Remember, it's the first impression that will often be the one that they take away with them.

Handshakes and Business Card Etiquette

Handshakes

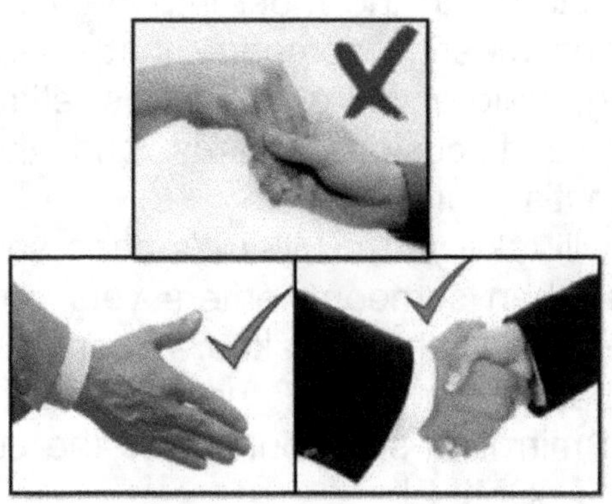

While it is good to give the other person a firm handshake, it is also important to note that 'firm' should not mean 'bone-crushing' but just comfortable enough for the other person. In other words your handshake should convey 'CARE'!

(Think of: **CAIR**- **C**onfidence, **A**ssurance, **I**nterest, **R**espect)

That is why we recommend that you practice the exact firmness of your handshake first with your own hand. This could be done by taking your left hand out: 4 fingers together and thumb up with the hand facing inwards towards you, as if it is a customers' hand. Now take your right hand the usual way you would use to shake someone's hand and assuming that your left hand is your customers' hand, shake as follows: Web into web first followed by the 4 fingers of your right hand around your left hand, with the thumb finally locking. Basically 3 locks...web into web, 4 fingers around and thumbs interlocked. Since it is your own hand, you will know what amount of firmness to use.

Keep practicing till you are comfortable with the right amount of firmness to clasp the other person's hand without it being 'bone-crushing' or the opposite- too limp (a dead fish hand shake!)

You can do this exercise whenever you are free, till you get accustomed to the exact amount of pressure to be used.

Now for some key points to remember while shaking hands:

A handshake can be initiated by either person and is appropriate when meeting a business associate in a social setting. Always stand when shaking someone's hand, and step out from behind a desk or table, while maintaining good eye contact and posture. A handshake should end by the time you have finished greeting the person. When meeting an elderly or disabled person, allow them to initiate the handshake.

Business Card Etiquette

When presenting business cards, they must always be presented face up with the front portion of the card facing towards the customer/guest, and if presenting with one hand as in most western countries then it must be held by the tip not covering any part of the text on the card.

Most Asian countries present cards with both hands. Whatever be the culture, please ensure the cards are never kept in a wallet as they would tend to get folded or bent at the edges or corner. All cards must be in pristine condition, crisp with no folds, wrinkles or soggy edges. Whenever presenting the card, make eye contact, with a pleasant smile.

Remembering Names

One of the most embarrassing moments when introducing people, would be when you mess up on their names. Remembering names may be difficult for some people, but it's not impossible. It's a skill: something that you can improve with constant practice and application.

Here are some ways to remember names:

- ✓ Repeat: When someone is introduced to you, repeat their name. *"It's a pleasure to meet you, John."* This can help reinforce your memory of the name. You may also introduce them to someone else so that you can create an opportunity to use their name.
- ✓ Use mental imagery: We think in pictures, therefore associating an image with a name can help in assisting recall. Imagine a

person's name written on their forehead. Pick an imagery that works for you. The more striking or exaggerated your mental picture, the bigger are the chances of recall.

- ✓ Put it on paper: Write the name down as soon as you can. Write their details on the business card they give you so that you would remember them the next time you see them around. (But make sure you don't let the person see you writing on their business card.)
- ✓ Be genuinely interested: Remembering names begin with attitude. If you are sincerely interested in a person, then they would make an impact on you. If you adapt the attitude that everyone is interesting, and are a potential ally in business, then remembering names would come as second nature.

Positive Introductions: Protocol, Rank, Status, Titles and Forms of Address

The first rule for introductions is that they be made. Don't get too worried about making a mistake during the introduction. Forgoing an introduction altogether, however, is a mistake that may leave a negative impression. Remember, as seen earlier, First Impressions create lasting Impressions. With that said, we must realize that the goal for making introductions is to provide information about each other so that there is a common ground to carry on a conversation. Introducing people is one of the most important acts we experience doing in our daily lives, yet very few people know how to do it correctly. Knowing how to make a graceful introduction will not only allow you to make a good impression but it will also give you the confidence and power to nurture these relationships from the get-go.

Studies have found that most people would rather have you ask for their names than to stand in a group and not be introduced. Another equally embarrassing scenario that often takes place is when it's 'assumed' two persons know one another and the introduction may go something like, "You two know one another." It is for this reason, at many business and/or social functions name badges are provided. They are given for the simple reason to help your memory.

To start, here are some important business introduction etiquette rules to remember:

There are five “S”s to a great introduction:

1. Smile.
2. Stand up straight.
3. See: make eye contact
4. Shake hands.
5. Say: “Hi! My name is ...and I don’t think we’ve met…

Arrival and Greetings when meeting someone

- ✓ As mentioned above, keep the 5S’s in mind
- ✓ Repeat the other person’s name in your greeting. Then say the name several times during the conversation
- ✓ Both men and women should be ready to initiate the handshake.
- ✓ Do not remove your jacket unless the host does. If you are uncomfortable, you may ask the host(s) permission to remove your jacket.
- ✓ It is considered acceptable for men to assist women with their chair but it does not always happen; in upscale restaurants, wait staff may assist.

- ✓ Another rule of thumb is that you're not expected when leaving an event to tour the entire room like a politician. It's always proper to say goodbye to those nearest to you and always seek out the host of the evening

When being Introduced

- ✓ When introducing yourself or when being introduced always stand and extend your right hand.
- ✓ If the person you're meeting is much older or a higher- level executive, say, *"I'm happy to meet you, Mr./ Ms. Name,'* or *"How do you do, Mr./ Mrs. Name,"*
- ✓ You may usually call younger people by their first names.
- ✓ If someone says, "How do you do," in response to an introduction, the proper response is, "How do you do" or "Pleased to meet you" and not 'fine thank you' as " How do you do" is a greeting, <u>not</u> a question.
- ✓ Say "I'm pleased to meet you" in response to an introduction. If you are being introduced, stand unless you are physically unable to.
- ✓ "Hello Mr./ Ms. Jackson. It's so very nice to meet you". Continue to use proper names when addressing your host until they give you permission to call them by their first name.
- ✓ If, however, you were introduced earlier in the evening and had some conversation, upon departure it is OK to say, "I'm glad to have met you Tom" Or, If you're on the receiving end of the farewell, reply "Thank you, Tom" or "I also enjoyed talking with you."
- ✓ If you are introducing more than one person, add a small amount of information about each

person (any mutual interests you are aware of, how you know them, or their occupation). This gives them a starting point for a conversation.
- ✓ Always have business cards on hand.

What do you say when you meet someone? Introducing Yourself

One of the most important ways to ensure you feel confident about speaking to others at networking events is to prepare a brief, engaging introduction. Your introduction should be fairly brief and should convey key pieces of information about you in a positive and interesting way.

This is called your Elevator Speech as it's a brief, persuasive speech that you can use to spark interest in a subject matter. How long should a good elevator pitch last? Picture a short elevator ride, around 20-30 seconds. Share the basics- Introduce yourself in one sentence (include your name, your background and your experience. What makes you unique-your interests, passions, skills, strengths, interests and aspirations? Demonstrate you skills- Talk about how you've used your strengths to overcome challenges and solve problems in the past- how you can benefit the other person, by indicating your greatest skill/area of expertise. Ask yourself "What/ where can I add value? Practice, practice, practice and practice some more! With practice your pitch will sound natural and you will grow more confident. Find the glue to link everything together – does it flow naturally

If you introduce yourself to another person, provide them with both your last and first names. The other person may have an easier time remembering your name if you give them a small piece of information about yourself on what you do etc.

Always have your Elevator Speech ready! Here are some examples:

Good Afternoon, I am Gerard Assey and the Founder CEO of a Group: 'Citius, Altius, Fortius Unlimited, specializing in Corporate Training, one of the divisions being the only one in this part of the World to be listed under the 'Who's Who of Training' and ranked as No.1 on all search engines!

Good morning, my name is Philip Joshua. My company, PJ Display Products, offers convenient, lightweight trade show displays to make your booth setup easier"

Now take a few minutes and work on preparing your own unique introduction!

When Introducing Others

- ✓ When you introduce someone, start with *"Mr. A, I'd like you to please meet Mr. B from Company / Dept / Location,"* or *Mrs. B, I'd like to introduce my sister, and C. C, this is Mrs. B."*
- ✓ Never phrase an introduction as a command*: "Mr. A, shake hands with / meet Ms. B."*
- ✓ Next, say something about the person being introduced: *"Ms. B works in our Marketing Division; or "John is a former neighbor of ours at (Location)."*
- ✓ This little bit of information to the group about the newcomer provides a topic of discussion so that the conversation can flow smoothly.
- ✓ Refrain however, from long stories about how you met, or about the person's life or background.
- ✓ Avoid phrases of superiority like *"John works for me"*

Protocol Business Etiquette when Introducing

- ✓ Generally, a lower ranked person in business is introduced to the higher ranked person - not vice versa. (Executives, clients, important guests would fall into the “higher ranked person” category.)
- ✓ When introducing a younger person to an older person (Use younger person’s first name, elder’s Last - about 15 years is the deciding point.) The name to say first is the Older person’s (“Ms. D, this is Jonny Alexander.”) Typically, someone younger is introduced to someone older.
- ✓ When a client is visiting, everyone in the office is introduced to the client first.
- ✓ When introducing a Peer in your firm to an outsider, the name to say first is the outsider's. When a peer from another company is introduced to a peer from your company, the person from your company is introduced to the person from the other company first.
- ✓ When introducing a non official to an official, always say the Officials name first
- ✓ When introducing a junior executive to a senior executive, always say the Senior Executive's name first.
- ✓ When introducing a company executive to a customer or a client, always say the clients name first
- ✓ A family member is introduced first to your boss.
- ✓ At an event with a guest of honor, all other guests are introduced first to the guest of honor.

- ✓ Always present the senior citizen, guest of honor, or dignitary first. Be sure to use titles, not first names, when introducing a much older person, a doctor (physician, psychologist, veterinarian, Ph.D.), a member of the clergy, or someone of official rank.
- ✓ Use a dignitary's title even if that person is retired and no longer holds that position: "Governor Singh," "Mayor Abraham," "Colonel Johnson," "Ambassador Kapoor."
- ✓ An obvious breach of etiquette is calling someone by a name you prefer, not the name they prefer. An unflattering nickname has no place in business .If Charles prefers to be called "Charles," that's what you should call him and how you should introduce him - not as "Charlie" or "Chuck." If you don't call him by the right name, or if you mispronounce his name, it's acceptable for Charles to correct you.
- ✓ If Charles prefers to be called "Chuckie boy," that's his business. Don't assume, however, that you know what people prefer.
- ✓ People are very sensitive about their names. Using incorrect names hurts your credibility and your chance of doing business with those you've misnamed.

Here are some examples that you can use to practice:

Situation 1 - Boss to Client

1. Introducer
2. Client: Mr. Samson
3. Your boss: Ms. Jackson

The introducer would say to the client, Mr. Samson, I'd like to introduce to you Ms. Jackson. Ms. Jackson is our Country Head. Mr. Samson is our client from Mauritius.

Situation 2 - Executive to a Client

1. Introducer
2. Office Manager: Susie Thomas
3. Client: Sanjay Kumar

The introducer would say to the client, Mr. Kumar, I'd like to introduce to you Susie Thomas. Ms. Thomas is our Sales Manager. Mr. Kumar is our client from Singapore

Situation 3- Junior Executive to Senior Executive

1. Introducer
2. Sr. Executive
3. Jr. Executive

The introducer would say to the Sr. Executive, Mr. Xxxx (Sr. Executive's name), I'd like to introduce to you Mr. Yyyy (Jr. Executive's name)

Overcoming Introduction Slip-ups

- ✓ Forgetting Names: Forgetting a person's name whom you have met before can happen to all of us and the worst thing you can do is to ignore them and not introduce them to your friends. The best thing to do is to apologize and say, "I am sorry, I know we have met but I can't remember your name." or say "I'm having a difficult time remembering your name." They should say their name and then you introduce everyone.
- ✓ Far ruder than forgetting a name, is not introducing people at all. People are usually very uncomfortable when they're not introduced as part of the group.

- ✓ When you're expecting several people and they are arriving separately, introduce each person as he or she arrives. Just politely interrupt the group's conversation and introduce the newcomer: "I'd like you all to meet Amanda Peters, the Communication Expert. Amanda, these are our associates from the southeastern office: Raj Sharma, Susan Abraham, and Mathew Thomas."
- ✓ If you're the one who's not introduced, take the initiative. Don't call attention and don't ask for an introduction. Just stand, extend your hand, smile and say, "Good Afternoon. I'm John Mathew, Mr. Fernando's Secretary and PA."
- ✓ If you are introduced but others are not, you may certainly take the initiative now, it's perfectly acceptable to start the conversation by introducing.
- ✓ There will be times when you do not remember everyone's name in the group- the best option in this case is to suggest that the people introduce themselves.
- ✓ If you are in a group and someone new walks up and no one introduces them, the polite thing to do is to stick out your hand and begin by saying your name. When this happens, it is a clue that the person you are with has forgotten the new person's name and can't introduce you.
- ✓ Not knowing one another: When you do not know if the people know one another, ask- "Have you met before?" If you are being introduced and the person

doing the introductions hesitates, fill in the introduction details.

Saying Good bye

- ✓ When escorting your guests back to the main exit, thank them for coming, shake each person's hand firmly, and make good eye contact.
- ✓ Just remember that the main rule of good manners in greeting people and making introductions is consideration for everyone.
- ✓ Even if you don't know the precise etiquettes, if you put people at ease and show proper respect, your actions will be acceptable.

Building and Managing Relationships

Networking as a key tool is all about relationships. It starts by thinking about different relationships we have or can make and how those relationships start to "weave a web" of networking. It will help them begin to realize how to use their current networks to broaden their future networks. After all, it's all about whom you know...who knows someone...and that who further knows someone else...and so on. And most of the time you are only 4 or 5 people away from anything you ever want or need. All you have to do is ask. So work to develop a core relationship with individuals who have influence in areas you aspire to grow.

There are 4 Key Components of Healthy Relationships- they are easily remembered as the 4C's:

Conditions: Creating a supportive environment in which the relationship can thrive (awareness, authenticity, respect, forgiveness, understanding and trust).

Connection: Working together in ways that improve each person and the ongoing relationship. The goal is for each person to contribute to the relationship and grow from the experience (engagement, empathy, mutuality, vitality and empowerment). For best results, colleagues and business partners need to feel connected, working towards a shared goal. This level of understanding encourages trust and openness, and nurtures acceptance and shared values. Connection takes time to develop, and not everyone realizes its importance. But you can build it through constant feedback, involving openness and appreciation.

Commitment: The same as with personal relationships, commitment means making a mindful and consistent decision to invest in a working relationship. In business, both sides need to work towards its growth. Some people don't need reminding about the need to do this, or how to go about it. But we can all do better.

Communication: Even if you've made a connection and you're committed to your plan, everyday business pressures can lead to communication problems. Talking openly to address and achieve what is important to the relationship and the individuals involved (candor, listening, inquiry and closure)

Let's look deeper into the 1st C- Creating & Sustaining CONDITIONS for Healthy Relationships

Healthy relationships don't just appear or survive on their own. Therefore, managers and supervisors must begin by creating and sustaining the conditions necessary for them to thrive. And there are five conditions that are listed below:

- ✓ Awareness – Both people are aware of how the relationship is doing, based on observations and experiences.
- ✓ Authenticity –If both people are being themselves, less time is spent pretending, and more time is spent attending to what is needed.
- ✓ Respect – Honor and value each person, and appreciate any differences.

- ✓ Flexibility – Create an environment in which there is room for people to make mistakes. No Blame/No Shame.
- ✓ Trust –Trust is the backbone

The 2nd C- The quality of the CONNECTION: How do they relate to each other?

The second component of healthy and productive relationships is the quality of the connection between the parties involved. How do the people relate to each other and what results from how they do so? Below are the key characteristics of healthy connection

- ✓ Engagement – Participation with integrity.
- ✓ Empathy – Stepping outside their views to see the world from another person's perspective.
- ✓ Mutuality – Being in balance with one another. Even in hierarchies it is important to recognize that learning and enrichment can occur in both directions.
- ✓ Vitality – A healthy relationship increases your energy and sense of being alive.
- ✓ Empowerment – Dedication to mutuality in the relationship. More is possible because of the relationship than without it.

How can we evaluate the quality of these Relationships?

If any one of these components is not present to a great degree, you need to consider how you will work to improve the relationship.

1) How engaged am I with the other person in this relationship?

2) How willing am I to stand in this person's shoes with empathy right now?

3) How much respect am I showing this person in this encounter?

4) How much am I in reciprocity and mutuality with this person?

5) How willing am I to increase their power as well as mine in this situation?

3rd C- COMMITMENT of every member in the Team

Just like a footballer who lets his team down by not showing up for matches, people who lack commitment at work can have a negative impact on their team's morale and performance. For this, every member must be willing to put in the time and effort needed if they want to achieve the organization's strategic priorities, by making sure to always keep their eyes on the prize. This will drive commitment in their personal efforts and set the right tone for building cultures of excellence for the people and organizations.

Here are some things that can help:

Team members feel Valued: When team members feel that their work is making a valuable contribution to the organization they will be more committed.

Purpose: Great teams have complete buy-in with their goals and objectives. They may go through a storming stage and can become disagreeable, but more often than not, this leads to better understanding and compromising on the best way of getting something done.

Alignment of Goals: Aligning team goals to company-wide goals is critical to demonstrate how each team's efforts contribute to the organization's success. Teams with goals that are not organizationally aligned often lose their sense of purpose over time. Likewise, when individuals' goals are aligned with their group's goals, team performance improves.

Clarity around Roles and Responsibilities: Ideally, each ones roles and responsibilities should be around their respective strengths and interests.

The Team is stretched: Team members are challenged enough and that they aren't bored. Those who are excited about projects they are working on at work will be more committed to their team and to the company.

Transparency and Openness: Leaders should ensure that their team's goals are visible and have been communicated to relevant parts of the organization. There is enough transparency that exists between top and lower level with opportunity to participate and contribute in various activities.

Give Praise where Praise is due: Praise leads to confidence and renewed energy, and can give team members the final push they need when faced with a difficult task.

Give people permission to fail: it's ok to fail and encourage team members to speak up if they spot any potential issues.

The 4th C- How people COMMUNICATE with each other

The fourth component of healthy relationships is how people communicate with each other. People in healthy relationships are able to have powerful conversations about things that matter to them, even when doing so is difficult.

Below are the characteristics of good communication:

Candor -Get the essential issues on the table and address them with honesty, clarity and respect. Say what you are thinking in ways that promote the conditions for a healthy relationship.

Listening- Take the time to truly hear the other person and their message with depth and respect.

Spaciousness- Make room for each person to express themselves

Enquiring- The other side of listening: being curious and seeking truth. Ask the right type of questions. Help others pursue their own answers.

Reconfirm- Make sure that both people are clear about what has been discussed and agreed to in a conversation

Communication is one of the main KEYS to Healthy Relationships.

Here are some other things that you can keep in mind to work on this area:

- ✓ Acknowledge/greet people with a smile
- ✓ Use polite gestures
- ✓ Maintain eye contact, as appropriate
- ✓ Maintain correct (upright, alert) posture
- ✓ Genuinely show interest in what others are saying
- ✓ Listen more, talk less
- ✓ Ask appropriate Questions-Open & Closed (More on this in another chapter)

Keys for Building Strong Relationships

Finally, what can you do to build Healthy and Strong Work Relationships? Here are some thoughts that can help you?

- ✓ Work on developing your people skills: Good relationships start with good people skills. In other words, how well you collaborate, communicate, commit and deal with conflict.
- ✓ Identify relationship needs: Look at the relationship needs of others as well as yourself. Do you know what they need from you? And do you know what you need from others? Understanding these needs can be instrumental in building better relationships
- ✓ Establish a set of values or 'ground rules' for yourself and apply them to every working relationship you develop: Adopt a consistent approach and aim to achieve the same degree of trust, respect and understanding with every person you work with.
- ✓ Respect Others: Respect others and their opinions. Never make others feel neglected, and not being harsh on their face when you disagree with them. Respect their inputs and try to explain your point of view with a little more empathy.
- ✓ Speak positively about the people you work with especially to your boss: Always speak positively to others and provide quality feedback about the people you work with. Shared information- positive or negative often comes back to the person being discussed. That will build trust.
- ✓ Listen Actively: Practice active listening when you talk to your customers and colleagues.

People respond to those who truly listen to what they have to say. Focus on listening more than you talk, and you'll quickly become known as someone who can be trusted.

- ✓ Set time aside to build relationships: Set a portion of your day towards relationship building, even if it's just a few minutes. Strengthen your relationships by aiming to get to know your colleagues better outside the workplace. Attend social events and group activities when you have the opportunity, to build rapport and spend time with your colleagues in a more relaxed setting. These little interactions help build the foundation of a good relationship, especially if they're face-to-face.
- ✓ Ask the people with whom you work most closely to provide you with some feedback on your working relationship and to highlight anything they might like you to do differently: Agree on steps you can both take to improve the relationship, if necessary.
- ✓ Learn to appreciate others: Show your appreciation whenever someone helps you. Everyone wants to feel that their work is appreciated. So, genuinely compliment the people around you when they do something well. This will open the door to great work relationships.
- ✓ Write thank-you notes: Write notes of appreciation to the people who are doing exemplary work, making positive contributions, and going above the call of duty. Everyone likes to be appreciated and will feel closer to you

- ✓ Be Positive: Focus on being positive. Positivity is attractive and contagious, and it will help strengthen your relationships with your colleagues. No one wants to be around someone who's negative all the time.
- ✓ Be proactive and help wherever you can without being asked: Where possible, offer your knowledge and experience to colleagues and find a way to help with work your colleagues are undertaking. Ask how you can get involved. This will form a closer connection because you are working directly with others to help them meet their goals. They will appreciate your support and get to know you better, which is vital to creating a more connected working relationship.
- ✓ Manage your boundaries: Make sure that you set and manage boundaries properly – all of us want to have friends at work, but, occasionally, a friendship can start to impact our jobs, especially when a friend or colleague begins to monopolize our time. If this happens, it's important that you're assertive about your boundaries, and that you know how much time you can devote during the work day for social interactions.
- ✓ Always keep your commitment and deliver as promised: Nothing is worse than someone who fails to deliver on a promise or consistently misses deadlines. There is no quicker way to spoil your reputation and damage potential working relationships than failing to follow through on work
- ✓ Never gossip: Totally avoid gossip. Office politics and "gossip" are major relationship

killers at work. If you're experiencing conflict with someone in your group, talk to them directly about the problem. Gossiping about the situation with other colleagues will only worsen the situation, and will cause mistrust and animosity between you.

- ✓ Identify someone within your professional network who has strong relationship-building skills (like a mentor) and ask them to coach or advise you on how you can improve your own approach to developing relationships.

Trust, Respect and Understanding- The 3 Key Pillars

Building Trust and the Measures of Trust

Robust communication is an essential part of trust in relationships.

Trust is the backbone for relationships. Without it, not much gets done well.

How to Build Trust?

The first job is to inspire trust. Trust is confidence born of 3 dimensions:

Character, Credibility and Competence

Character includes your integrity, motive, and intent with people.

Competence includes your capabilities, skills, abilities, results, and track record. Both dimensions are vital.

The foundation of trust is your own Credibility, and it can be a real differentiator. When a leader's credibility and reputation are high, it enables them to establish trust fast - speed goes up, cost goes down.

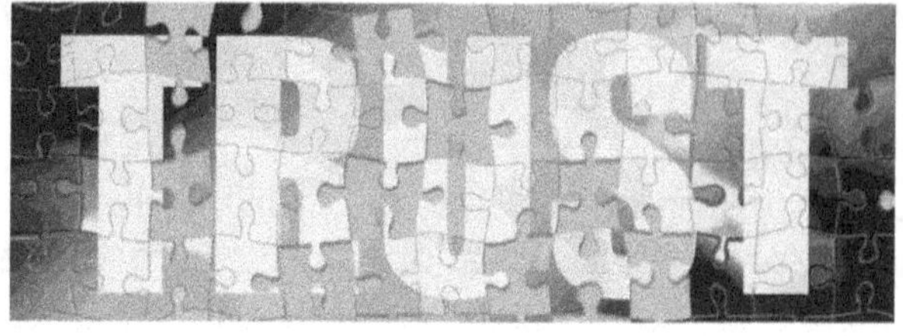

5 Common Measures of Trust

- ✓ Reliability: I trust that if I give this assignment to Rani, she will get it done on time.
- ✓ Candor: I trust that if I ask Raja for his feedback on my proposal before I submit it that he will be honest and constructive with me.
- ✓ Safety: I trust that if I share my struggles as a new manager with my peer she will respond with empathy and keep it confidential.
- ✓ Competency: I trust that if I ask Tom to present our group's report in my absence he will do a great job.
- ✓ Integrity: I trust that Rani will keep her word in the agreement we just made about her work.

How to Build Credibility and Trust

- ✓ Set a good example
- ✓ Keep commitments
- ✓ Tell the truth
- ✓ Be fair
- ✓ Don't have favorites
- ✓ Admit mistakes
- ✓ Be well-informed
- ✓ Understand the issues
- ✓ Share information
- ✓ Show respect

Building Respect

A mutual respect between individuals should underpin all working relationships. Demonstrating respect is fundamental to gaining trust and will form the foundations of a relationship in which ideas and opinions can be shared openly. Respect can be earned in a number of ways:

- ✓ Treat one another as equals. Even in relationships in which individuals have different levels of organizational seniority, colleagues should treat each other equally. 'Pulling rank' can make others in the relationship feel less valued.
- ✓ Share your knowledge with your colleagues. Offer them the benefit of your experience and encourage them to do the same.
- ✓ Recognize the achievements of others and make them aware that you value the contribution they make to your working relationship.
- ✓ Be honest. Committing to unrealistic time frames or making promises that can't be kept can be very damaging to working relationships. Be upfront with your colleague if you face constraints on time or resources, and suggest an alternative solution that is more achievable.

Understanding Others

Taking the time to understand your colleagues can be of real benefit to your working relationships. This means taking the time to learn what motivates and drives them to achieve their goals. Understanding can be developed in a number of ways, for example:

- ✓ Arranging an introductory meeting when you start working with someone for the first time to establish what you can expect from one another in the working relationship.
- ✓ Establishing shared objectives when embarking upon a new project or initiative to allow you to work towards a common goal.

- ✓ Using active listening skills during meetings and discussions. Active listening means listening intently to what someone is saying and making it clear to them throughout that you have heard and understood them.
- ✓ Finding out what each others' strengths are so you can agree on how best to share responsibilities when approaching tasks together.

Asking the Right Questions and Listening are the KEYS!

To establish rapport with someone new, it is important to ask some well-considered questions once you have introduced yourself. The purpose of this isn't to interrogate the other person, but to find out more about them and spark a more in depth conversation. Depending on your reasons for networking, and the purpose of the event you're attending, you may wish to ask the other person about their role and responsibilities, their professional background, and why they were first drawn to the event.

Learning to ask better questions in our everyday conversations has enormous benefits on relationships. Firstly, asking appreciative questions improves one's emotional intelligence and demonstrates empathy to the receiver of your question. Also, asking well-considered questions expands the possibilities in the answer and has the potential to deepen a relationship.

However, sadly, we are biased towards telling instead of asking, because we live in a pragmatic, problem-solving culture in which knowing things and telling others what we know is valued .In order to build relationships based on dialogue and mutual respect, it is essential to learn to ask more questions. This shows care and concern.

Questions are a powerful tool to nurture relationships and make them effective and satisfactory for both sides.

If we start asking more questions we will immediately notice the benefits in our relationships with others:

- ✓ We'll understand the **people** we are relating to
- ✓ We'll focus on them and encourage **empathy**
- ✓ We'll allow them to express themselves and give us the **information** we want
- ✓ We'll stimulate their **attention** and their involvement
- ✓ It would indicate that we care and are genuinely concerned.

In order that the communicative exchange is effective and that the dialogue is fluid, it is important to ask the right question, and in order to ask our questions in an effective way, we should ask ourselves "*What do I want to obtain? What do I really need to know?*" this way the exchange of information can go straight to the point

So the art of asking the right questions requires the use of different types of questions. First let us have an understanding of the different types of questions that we could ask someone. Though there are several types of questions, for the purpose of this exercise let us look at just the 3 most important ones ie;

OPEN Questions

CLOSED Questions

FOLLOW-UP Questions

Depending on what type of answer you want from the other person, either of these questions are used.

Eg; If I asked you: *'Did you have your dinner'?*

Or *'Do you like this training session?'* or *'Are you going home this evening'?*

The only possible answer that you could give me would either be a *'yes'* or a *'no'*

That is why this type of question is called a 'closed question', because the only possible answer would be a one word- with either a *'yes'* or *'no'*

Closed questions usually begin with:

'Are you...'

'Will you...'

'Do you...'

'Would you...'

They are usually not very helpful in starting a conversation and extracting information. However, most people are more comfortable asking such questions.

The opposite of 'closed' is the obvious: 'open'. Open questions allow the other person to open up or do the talking and are used to encourage the other side to speak freely about a concern or expand on something already raised during the conversation.

Always remember this: Open questions generally begin with 5W's and 1 H ie;

Who?

What?

When?

Where?

Why?

How?

And they encourage the other person to open up and speak.

If we were to redo that example again using open questions, they would go something like this: *'What did you have for dinner?' 'How do you feel about this training?' 'What plans do you have for this evening'?*

These questions will certainly not fetch you a *'yes'* or *'no'* like how closed questions do. But they would allow the other person to open up with information which is what we could be looking forward to, by asking such questions.

Shooting out these questions without any logical order would also be inappropriate, as it could be unprofessional, could be irritating at times and most of all cause confusion in the mind of the other person. But if the other person was taken through a logical pattern, it could help lead him or open up to making the conversation two-way and interesting for both parties

Effective listening involves the use of follow-up questions and they are useful in several ways:

- ✓ They show we are interested and encourage the other person to keep talking.
- ✓ They increase the quality of the information gained.
- ✓ They help us to confirm our understanding of what has been said.

Before we can ask a follow-up question we need to listen to what the other side has said and wait for an appropriate pause in the conversation to ask the question.

Follow-up questions can also take the form of a question asked in response to a statement by the other side. They can reflect the information in the original question by beginning with phrases like:

So you are saying that...?

Does that mean...?

If I understand correctly are you saying that...?

Followed by a summary of what was said by the customer.

Let us see some examples now!

Examples of Open questions:

What exactly do you see the issue as Tim?

How can I help you solve this problem?

These Questions can help to dig into or search for details and are also called Probing Questions:
"Exactly how did this happen?"
"What steps did you take?"

Examples of Closed questions:

Did you receive the letter we sent you on Friday?
Are you happy with the service you have received?

Examples of Follow up questions:

What were you told when you rang us?
How quickly were you promised a reply?

In these examples the follow-up questions have been asked in response to the customer saying that he
1) Rang us previously,
2) Was told he would be given a reply

Listening Skills

Now while the other person talks, you would need to listen attentively.

'People were designed with two ears and one mouth, and that is the ratio in which to use them'!

How to be a good listener?

One of the greatest skills that one can develop is the skill of listening. The best professionals are the ones that do less talking and more of listening and that is why I believe God gave us two ears and one mouth- so we would do more listening than talking!

Listen Actively

- ✓ Focus on the speaker
- ✓ Keep an open mind
- ✓ Tolerate silence
- ✓ Ask open-ended questions
- ✓ Repeat the speaker's thoughts
- ✓ Listen for facts and key words

To be an "active" listener:

- ✓ Suspend judgment, initially

- ✓ Avoid distractions; when on the telephone don't carry on side conversations; when face-to-face make eye contact
- ✓ Assess what you heard
- ✓ Clarify and confirm
- ✓ Take notes of key points
- ✓ Never use your phone in the customer's premises! It's a big disturbance and bad manners!

Before you respond, assess the information you heard by asking yourself four questions:

- ✓ What has he/she told me?
- ✓ What can I do with this information?
- ✓ What else do I need to know?
- ✓ What questions do I still need to ask?

To show you're listening actively:

- ✓ Use terms like, 'Go on', Uh huh' and 'mmm'
- ✓ Stay tuned in/Watch for non-verbal cues

To show that you have, understood:

- ✓ Use, phrases like "I see," "I understand"
- ✓ Paraphrase, "So you want me to ..."

Clarifying what they said:

In order to more fully understand what is being said we can make it clearer by asking for more detail:

- ✓ *You said that you were not satisfied with our service...Can you tell me why?*
- ✓ *You mentioned how helpful we had been. Can you elaborate specifically In what way?*
- ✓ *You said there had been problems in the past. What were they like?*

Clarifying and Reconfirming with Closed Questions

This is the time when closed questions are very useful. To clarify and reconfirm, restate in your own words what the other person has said and ask him/her to verify your understanding. An example would be: *'Mr Customer, Let me just take a minute to summarize, just to ensure that I've got the right information...You were mentioning that you were having a problem with....Am I right Mr. So & So?"*

After the other person has confirmed your understanding, you have earned the right to proceed with additional questions to gain more information about the situation.

Why summarize regularly?

- ✓ *It keeps complexities under control*
- ✓ *It tests progress*
- ✓ *It lets you restate what the other party has said*
- ✓ *It can help gain the initiative*
- ✓ *It can keep the discussion on track*
- ✓ *It can prevent misinterpretation, misunderstanding and subsequent bitterness*
- ✓ *In other words, summarizing helps you stay on top (but you take the point).*

By summarizing, you are making sure you have the right information and that you haven't left out anything.

Key Strategies and Steps to Successful Networking

The Key Strategies and Steps to Networking Successfully

The best place to network is to begin in your comfort zone, and most of the time you are only 4 or 5 people away from anything you ever want or need. But all you have to do is ask. Work to develop a core relationship with individuals who have influence in areas you aspire to grow. There are basically 3 key stages in Networking: Before, During and After the Event

Before the Event

Step 1: You must have an Objective: Before attempting to network-online or in-person, it's important to resolve in your mind the question of why. Think about what you want to achieve from networking. Do you want to develop your career, meet new clients and collaborators, broaden your horizons, or all of the above? Networking is much more productive and enjoyable when you have a clear goal in mind. Where do you see yourself in the next three, five, and ten years. What's your outlook for the future?

Why are you doing this? What's your agenda? What is your objective of networking? What are the likely groups that you could get into? Who do you need to talk to? Target people/organizations? What do you want to achieve or find out? Where do you hope it will lead you?

How could you contact them?

- ✓ Looking up their profile
- ✓ Networking at events
- ✓ Asking connections

Simply waiting for people to contact you, will only give you a fraction of the benefits that reaching out to new or existing contacts can offer. Setting yourself a stretching, but achievable target can be a helpful way of making sure you remain proactive. Examples of relevant targets could include 'I will attend two networking events next month', or 'I will arrange catch-up meetings with five of my existing contacts this quarter'. Go with a specific outcome in mind. Set a specific objective for the networking event. For example, "I'm going to meet five prospective new employers/clients tonight."

The best networkers know that there's some work involved in order to be prepared to make a positive impression and walk away with a few meaningful connections.

Step 2: Your Comfort Zone: Your comfort zone will be in the areas you know, namely: what you want, who and where you are

- ✓ Your Agenda
- ✓ Your Story
- ✓ Your Questions

- ✓ Your Conversations
- ✓ Your Connection Points

How do you begin to Network? Start simple: who do you already know that can help? Friends and Family, Class/ College mates, Advisors and Professors, Former Work Colleagues, Events, Conferences, Professional Association Meets, Chambers of Commerce Meets, Career Fairs, Alumni Mentor Networks, Leveraging Friends on Platforms like Facebook , Twitter, LinkedIn etc

Begin by identifying what and who you know

What you know:

- ✓ What are you selling and who are your target customers? What is your core message? What do you want prospective employers to know about you, your background, your experience, your accomplishments? How are you marketing yourself to prospective employers? Sometimes, this core message gets crafted into a summary of qualifications and used at the beginning of a resume. More importantly, it serves as the litmus test for all information you put about yourself, share with networking contacts, or use in an interview.
- ✓ Consider: Defining the level of position you are seeking or the specific type of business partner/ contact/lead. How you can benefit the employer/ contact/ business partner with your greatest skill/area of expertise. Think "Where/What value can I add"?

Identify who you know.

- ✓ Try to come up with a list of at least 15 people you would consider as strong contacts; people who know you and whom you believe would be willing to offer you advice and assistance.

Start with these 15 personal/ professional contacts. If each of those 15 contacts introduces you to three additional people you will have 45 contacts.

If each of those 45 contacts introduces you to three additional people, you will have 135 contacts. And, if each of those 135 contacts introduces you to three additional people, you will have 405 total contacts. The process may not be quite that mathematically clean and easy, but you get the picture as an example.

Who are your strong ties? They might be: Family Members Friends/Colleagues of Family Members. Current/Former Professors, Parents of Friends, Internship Supervisors, Fellow Colleagues now in new jobs, Neighbors, Professional Association/ Chambers of Commerce Members, Your Pastor/Priest/Church Leader, Current/Former Bosses, College Alumni

Step 3: Make a start by joining the Networking Groups you decided on in the earlier step. One recommended way to begin networking is to join at least two organizations. One networking group related to your target market and another of your peers. The target market group will allow you to meet people who you would like to work with and promote your business, whereas the peer group is for gathering knowledge in your field by hanging out with others like yourself.

Step 4: Do your Preparation (This step is very important)

If attending an event, research the event. Call or contact the organizers to find out as much information as possible and identify speakers and attendees. Casually reach out beforehand if appropriate, for example by following speakers on social media. Get to know what the event will be like. Ask questions such as: How many people do they expect to attend? What is the format and dress code? Identify your personal strategy and set goals for the event as we've already discussed. Prepare your specific 'attention-grabbing' statements to answer the questions *"Who are you and what do you do?"*

Do your Homework on the Networking Group/ Event!

Things to do BEFORE the networking meeting or event:

1. Get a list of attendees
   - ✓ Ask the host or facilitator
   - ✓ Enquire online
2. Search for attendee's websites
   - ✓ Gather information
   - ✓ Review company services
   - ✓ Look at their picture
3. Select the people you want to meet
   - ✓ Write down their names
   - ✓ Call them before the event
   - ✓ Seek them out at the event
4. Ask the host or facilitator to introduce you to 2 or 3 people
   - ✓ People who would typically be a referral source
   - ✓ People who may be a potential client
   - ✓ People who are mover's and shaker's
5. Be updated on happenings/ policies/ news in your domain

   Read that day's newspaper- Read the local newspaper before an event to find five or six current event topics you can bring into a conversation

Think about:

- ✓ What do you want to find more out about?
- ✓ How are you going to bring these questions into conversations?

Step 5: You must have a compelling Story: Your Elevator Speech (See more on this in another earlier chapter) How do you present yourself in different contexts? And this can often be the most difficult part of any event-how to introduce yourself to strangers.

Your goal should be something like:

1. Introduce yourself to the people in your core group
2. Ensure that people in this core group know what specialty and industry you are in. Prepare your specific 'attention-grabbing' statements to answer the questions "Who are you and what do you do?"

Step 6: Things to bring to the meeting or event:

- ✓ An Impressive Leather Briefcase/ Handbag
- ✓ Your Company Brochures/ PowerPoint presentation on Laptop (or other device)
- ✓ Have plenty of Business Cards with you (at least 100). You can even have two versions- one with your mobile number on it, and one without, if you don't necessarily want everyone to have your direct number. You can also think of having your business cards outlining your value proposition
- ✓ Place business cards in your left pocket
- ✓ Name badges (if applicable)

Step 7: What Impression do you want to create: Your first 30 Seconds Count!

"You only get one chance to make a <u>first</u> good impression."

First Impressions (More on this in an earlier chapter)

- ✓ Dress for the Occasion: 60% of people are visual communicators. This means that to 60% of the world-image is key.
- ✓ Demeanor: Business entrance should be professional and quite seamless and understated.
- ✓ Introductions: Person of higher rank receives the introduction. Use the name of higher-ranking person first.
- ✓ Handshake and Share Business Card (See more on these in an earlier chapter)
- ✓ Get there early and stay late
- ✓ Introduce yourself within 60 seconds of entering the room

During the Event

Step 8: Working your way around in the Event

- ✓ Meet new contacts. Do not hang with people you know. Meet people you want to do business with. It is not a card gathering experience
- ✓ Look for groups of 2 or 3 people. Get into groups already formed
- ✓ An easy way to introduce yourself to a group is *"Do you mind if I join your conversation?"*
- ✓ Entering a Group, if you are on the outside: If the conversation appears personal or intense, find a different group; Look for a physical gap, stand nearby and make eye contact; After you have been acknowledged, join the conversation; Listen to the conversation and find a way to contribute- don't dominate.
- ✓ See more details on making conversations in the next chapter
- ✓ If you are already in a group: Help others join the conversation; Make eye contact and move

over to allow space for him/her to join the group; During a lull in the conversation, introduce yourself and others to the new person.

- ✓ If approaching a speaker or any other group official have something relevant to ask e.g. *'I thought X part of your paper was really interesting, in particular I wanted to ask about...'*

Step 9: Seek information first

- ✓ Get others to reveal their wants and needs
- ✓ Let others shine and feel good about themselves
- ✓ Make others believe that you are listening and are interested
- ✓ Look at the other person for approximately 60% of the time. Give plenty of eye-contact but be careful not to make them feel uncomfortable.
- ✓ When listening, nod and make encouraging sounds and gestures.
- ✓ Use the other person's name early in the conversation. This is not only seen as polite but will also reinforce the name in your mind so you are less likely to forget it! If they have an unusual name remark about it *"Wow! That's an unusually lovely name I don't think I've heard it before"* or ask them to spell it out. Say goodbye using their name.
- ✓ Smile!
- ✓ Try to ask the other person open questions- the type of questions that require more than a yes or no answer. (More on this in an earlier chapter)
- ✓ Avoid contentious topics of conversation.

- ✓ Use feedback to summarize, reflect and clarify back to the other person what you think they have said. This gives an opportunity for any misunderstandings to be rectified quickly.
- ✓ Talk about things that refer back to what the other person has said. Find links between common experiences.

Step 10: Give your "elevator speech"

- ✓ Reveal how you can help them
- ✓ Briefly explain what you do and how you do it
- ✓ Build their curiosity and interest in you
- ✓ Be enthusiastic about your business when asked- When people ask you what you do, be excited and passionate about it. If you aren't, don't expect anyone else to be.

Step 11: Conversation conclusions:

Exiting a Conversation Gracefully

Avoid the comfort of talking exclusively with people you already know. Don't spend more than 10 minutes with any single person. When exiting-smile, make eye contact, and say something positive in closing; you may shake hands too.

Good moments for you to exit are when others enter a conversation or when you introduce someone else into the conversation. Don't feel the need to justify your exit- the point of the event is to talk to multiple people.

If you want to do business, conclude your conversation with offers and requests

- ✓ Send follow-up materials
- ✓ Introduce them to a colleague
- ✓ Ask for a business card (Try and put something personal/ key information at the back of the card like "travelled from Malaysia for conference". But not in front of them!)

- ✓ Possible phrases for exiting include: *"I've enjoyed talking with you."* or *"Thanks for talking with me. I hope we can talk more later." "I've enjoyed talking with you, but I don't want to take up any more of your time." "Is it alright if I contact you in the future? And if I can be of help to you- please let me know."*

  Say something like *"It seems as though it would be worth following up with a more specific discussion. Would you be open to meeting up after the conference?"* or *"I will call you tomorrow and see if we can help each other, okay?"* Or, you could close a conversation by saying *'It has been great to find out more about you. What is the best way to contact you in future?'*

  If they agree to a meeting see if you can schedule it right then and there with your smart phone and ask if they have theirs.

If you do not want to do business, conclude your conversation:

- ✓ Do not exchange business cards
- ✓ Use *the great escape* exit: *"I have enjoyed meeting you and I look forward to seeing you again."*
- ✓ Or to make a graceful exit. *"I have to make a quick call"*, or *"I'm going to get a drink of water if you'd excuse me?"* or *"I just spotted someone else I need to speak to, lovely to meet you."* or *"I've enjoyed meeting you. I know you have others you would like to meet and so would I . . ."*

After the Event

Step 12: After the Event

Take time to write notes on the back of (their) business card or by using the Contacts App on your phone. Review notes you have made. Follow up quickly to get the best results. The best networkers are the people who actually work at networking. They meet people, they take notes, they follow up the very next day, they build relationships-they get the business.

- ✓ Write a quick note or send an email: remind them that you met them at the event and what you spoke about. Send it soon after the event (within 24 hours). Keep it simple and friendly
- ✓ Connect on LinkedIn after- Personalize your connection request using the notes you put on the back of the new contact's business card
- ✓ Send an article or useful resource-A relevant article, important telephone number or website. Make sure it is simple and helpful
- ✓ Send a thank-you note for suggestions, ideas, and resources resulting from your contact. Show appreciation
- ✓ Do them a favor. Introduce them to associates, clients and vendors. Help them to achieve their goals
- ✓ Send them a referral. Ask for a follow-up call
- ✓ Send a gift. Make it appropriate, and always add a note
- ✓ Keep contacts on your mailing list. Use a contact management software for tracking
- ✓ Remember: Persistence pays

Step 13: Always give something back to your network.

- ✓ Be Giving: Give your time, your resources, your advice, and especially your referrals.

- ✓ Stay positive. It will all come back to you in a positive manner in the end. Think about what a person may remember after meeting you.

Step 14: Seek a Mentor-Mentoring can help you with many aspects.

- ✓ A good mentor can help with one-to-one communication and helps you work towards clear, agreed objectives that can be an invaluable asset to your career or business.
- ✓ However, it is important to be clear about where the role of the mentor begins and ends.

Name Placement Tags or Badges

Name badges are always worn on the right hand side of your front shoulder area. Why? The reason is that as you extend your hand in greeting, the gaze of the person you are meeting can easily follow your extended arm back allowing for a natural progression for the eyes to the name tag.

Some Other Good Tips Include:

- ✓ Arrive early. Arriving before the venue is noisy and full of people lets you get accustomed to the sights and sounds of the room before they become overwhelming. You can also scope out places to retreat to if you need a moment of solitude.
- ✓ Arrive with a friend or colleague. Not knowing anyone can be uncomfortable. Walking in with a friend guarantees you will know at least one person in the room who can introduce you to others.
- ✓ Have strategies to re-energize mid-event. Give yourself a networking time limit and then go somewhere to regroup in solitude. Or

consider taking a break to peruse the display items on the table/shelf or elsewhere. Sometimes you just need to be seen and not heard.

Rules for Business Introductions

- ✓ Know the status and rank
- ✓ Know the first and last names
- ✓ Pronounce each person's name correctly
- ✓ Know some piece of relative information
- ✓ Knowledge of person's job
- ✓ Use formal, academic or political title before last name
- ✓ Mr., Mrs., or Ms.
- ✓ Use formal introductions for senior-ranking executives
- ✓ Repeat person's name
- ✓ Name Tags do not replace proper introductions

And Finally…Some Deadly Networking Mistakes

- ✓ Hanging around your friends
- ✓ Staying too long in one group
- ✓ Being too busy- only eating and drinking
- ✓ Talking nonstop
- ✓ Asking about the weather or other irrelevant topics
- ✓ Getting pushy about meeting socially
- ✓ No follow-up or follow-through

The Right Networking Conversations

You have very little time to make a good first impression. We had seen in an earlier chapter on how to handle that first 30 seconds, the social ritual part- shaking hands and introducing yourself. Now you must build on that first impression- you have to make that person feel good about being with you, even for a brief encounter.

According to studies, 75% of us feel awkward and shy when we meet new people and find it difficult to start a conversation with a stranger. People are afraid of being rejected, or saying the wrong thing or just not fitting into the group.

Here are a few thoughts for ensuring the right conversations at Lunches/ Dinners

- ✓ Reflect on why you are there. Consider the purpose/context of the dining experience. Is it part of a job interview process? A formal or informal gathering of co-workers? A business deal? A major project or sale? A partnership deal?
- ✓ Come prepared accordingly: Remember that business dining is all about conversation. So come prepared with appropriate dinner conversation. You need to contribute to your table talk in a way that sets other dinner guests at ease. So do all your research in advance. Who will be attending? What interests might they have? What topics are in line with the focus of the function? When the inevitable lapse in conversation occurs, know leading questions that will encourage table

guests to begin talking about themselves. Questions or statements such as: “I’m interested in knowing a little about the kind of work you do.” “Please tell me about your interest in the organization represented here.” “Have you heard the speaker before?”

✓ Be well informed

- What are the current events for today? Do you have small talk options ready for the function, if needed?
- Read at least one daily newspaper and a weekly news magazine
- Before going to an event, read the headlines of the day. Current events are perfect for small talk. And don't forget the sports and arts pages.
- Bring up these topics during the first conversational lull; the other person will be grateful for your filling the silence and will most likely follow your lead.

✓ Be Curious: It’s not about you. Try focusing more on the other person.

✓ Wait for the host to initiate a discussion: Generally, the host initiates the business discussion. Business, if not urgent, is often discussed toward the end of the meal or over coffee. If you are the host, it's your job to steer the conversation, to suggest topics for discussion, and to make sure that everyone at the table is given the opportunity to be part of the general conversation. When the table isn't involved in a general discussion, be a good conversationalist with the people seated on either side of you.

- ✓ Pay attention to the thread of conversation and participate when appropriate. Don't interrupt or repeatedly turn the topic of conversation to you or your interests.
- ✓ Take a glance at the person to see if there is anything about them that could start a conversation. People will be flattered by and appreciate your interest in them.
- ✓ If you're at a concert, trade meet- talk about the group, the room, food, entertainment. The same goes for wherever you may be.
- ✓ Try to choose universal topics of conversation in which all may have an interest. If you can't think of anything to say, then just listen attentively, and ask questions to generate conversation.
- ✓ Ask them appropriate, relevant questions about themselves-to start the conversation. Listen actively and show appreciation as they speak. Your conversation partner feels important when you ask questions; people like to talk about themselves, so let them do it.
- ✓ When you ask questions, there is a lot less pressure for your partner- you are perceived as caring, open and humble. Be a good listener! Ask OPEN ENDED questions that lead to longer answers. These types of questions usually ask who, what, when, where, why, and how, and use verbs that deal with your senses. (Covered separately under a different chapter)
  What do you think of…?
  How do you know so and so…?
  What got you into…?
  What gave you the idea…?

Describe….tell me about.

It's a good idea to prepare some questions before you go to an event. That way you'll have something to fall back on.

- ✓ Now share brief, reflective relevant comments about yourself if asked.
- ✓ Have only one conversation at a time
- ✓ Don't dominate the table. Give everyone a fair share to speak. And remember that you are responsible for conversing with your "triangle."

Conversing with your "Triangle"

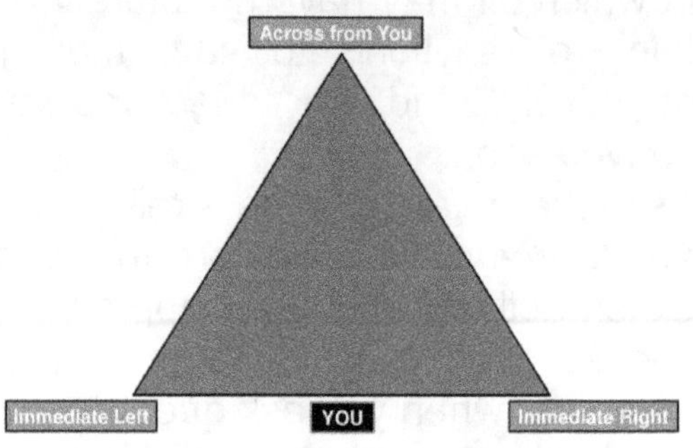

- ✓ Pay attention to people's physical needs. Do they need another drink? Something more on their plate?
- ✓ Avoid a loud tone of voice. Do not use profanities. Be sensitive to others before initiating conversation on topics that may not be suitable- avoid anything of a vulgar, graphic, or otherwise unpleasant nature. Ensure the conversation is entirely free of controversial subjects-Never tell jokes, as you never know who you could offend.
- ✓ If you are someone else's guest, even if part of a group, don't criticize the food, restaurant,

etc. - this can cause embarrassment on the part of the "host."

- ✓ Food is secondary! Your focus should be on having good conversations. Never talk with food in your mouth or chew with your mouth open. Select easy foods to eat— avoid sticky foods and messy sauces. If you are at a standing reception, you should either have a drink or a plate—not both! Hold the cup/ drink in your left hand, leaving your right hand free to greet people

Starting a conversation

A good place to start is to think of common interests. For starting a conversation or breaking the ice with strangers, think of: F.O.R.M.

F-Family

O-Occupation

R-Recreation

M-Money (economy)

Small talk can be a real saver in many situations. It fills the voids in conversations, helps ease tense moments, sets others at ease, and helps one become acquainted with others. There are two ways to make initiating small talk a little easier.

- ✓ The first is to be well-informed. To be able to discuss topics such as current best-selling books, news events, famous people, fitness crazes, technological advances, travel, and sports. These are all appropriate small talk subjects.
- ✓ The second way to ease into small talk is by asking others about themselves, their family, work, or hobby.

Here are some topics that are appropriate to speak up and get you started:

Small Talk Topics

- ✓ Your location or venue
- ✓ Shows, movies, plays, etc
- ✓ Art
- ✓ Food, restaurants, or cooking
- ✓ Their hobbies
- ✓ Their professional interests and responsibilities
- ✓ Sports
- ✓ The climate
- ✓ Travel
- ✓ Their local shopping favorites

Good Topics

- ✓ Current events, news etc
- ✓ Emerging Trends, Best Practices (Eg. How's business been amidst recession/ challenge etc?)
- ✓ Career Journeys + Performance/Burn Out Advice
- ✓ Food
- ✓ Memberships
- ✓ Mutual friends
- ✓ Hobbies
- ✓ Industry talk
- ✓ Styles/ Trends
- ✓ Sports

Bad Topics

- ✓ Any personal issues such as: family, health/ illnesses/ divorces/ separation/ affairs etc which may trigger something
- ✓ Religion/ religious beliefs
- ✓ Politics
- ✓ Salaries/ financial situation

- ✓ The cost of things
- ✓ Off color jokes- Racial, ethnic, and sexually oriented jokes
- ✓ Gossip
- ✓ Weight, height, shoe size, age or mental health

Helpful Small Talk Topics-During a Conference/ Event

- ✓ Offer a genuine compliment, such as, *"I really enjoyed your presentation. Can you tell me more about your research/ paper?"*
- ✓ Talk about the event itself, such as: *"Is this your first time attending this conference?" "What session have you most enjoyed so far?"*
- ✓ Small talk is frequently about personal interests and hobbies, such as: "*What do you do in your spare time?" "Have you been doing much travelling lately?"*

Here are some ways of opening a conversation for various situations:

For Prospects/ Customers:

- ✓ What were some of the key initiatives you took that brought you this far?
- ✓ What makes you stand out from your competitor?
- ✓ What's the most exciting thing about your business?
- ✓ What's the most exciting thing about your team?
- ✓ What are some of the most significant changes in your industry in recent years?
- ✓ If you could go back one year in time, what would you do differently?

- ✓ I'm honestly curious to know your story
- ✓ Tell me about your...?
- ✓ What's your company's biggest priority right now?
- ✓ How has business changed since we talked last?
- ✓ How are your efforts in [related business area]?
- ✓ What can I do to help you achieve….?

Common event

- ✓ What do you think of the conference so far? ... How have the sessions been? What did you particularly like?
- ✓ What inspired you to become a member of this body?

Company/Job

- ✓ Tom mentioned of how you were recently given additional responsibilities…Congratulations!
- ✓ How do you like this new role? What are some of the new areas responsibilities now? How different is it to what you were doing?

Business/Industry

- ✓ Off what I know, you were all along into production? How and what made you get into this active sales role?
- ✓ How have the recent changes in the government regulations affecting your business?

Location

- ✓ I live in Delhi. Where are you from?
- ✓ This is my very first visit to Mauritius. What do you recommend I see while I'm here?
- ✓ What is it that you like about living in Colombo?

Sports

- ✓ I hear that your favorite past time is playing golf. Did you see the xxxx Cup this year?
- ✓ Last night's cricket match kept me in real suspense. What did you feel about it?

Travel

- ✓ Sarah was mentioning that you just returned from Turkey. How was your trip?
- ✓ I know you'd been to Israel recently. Our family is also planning a trip sometime next year. How do you recommend we go about this?

Hobbies/Interests

- ✓ I noticed that you volunteered in the company's cancer prevention drive? That's certainly a good deed to do. How did the event go?
- ✓ What are your hobbies or interests outside of work?

For Job Applicants

Sample questions to ask during an informational interview/ chat:

- ✓ What do you do at this company?
- ✓ What is the best part of your job?
- ✓ What type of education or training is necessary to do this type of job?
- ✓ What other types of jobs are there at this company?
- ✓ Can you tell me more about this company?
- ✓ How do you apply for a job at this company?
- ✓ Can you look at my resume and give me some feedback on it

Some Common Conversation Killers

How do you know if a question is too personal? Ask yourself how you would feel if someone asked you the question and everybody in the room could hear the answer. If you'd feel comfortable, the question is OK.

Avoid:

- ✓ Bragging
- ✓ Interrupting
- ✓ Monopolizing
- ✓ Not playing the game

If someone asks a question, give him or her something to work with. Don't do this: *"How was your vacation?' "Fine"*

Instead*: "How .was your vacation?" "Fine The beach was great and we went boating every day."*

With your Boss

When you are out with your boss for lunch or dinner...

Here are a few points you can keep in mind while on a dinner/lunch with your boss.

- ✓ Focus on your attire-Dress Professionally
- ✓ Be punctual and on time
- ✓ Be active and enthusiastic all the time
- ✓ Watch your body language and mannerisms
- ✓ Maintain a presence of mind and positive attitude
- ✓ Let your host take the lead
- ✓ Stay focused
- ✓ Pick appropriate topics- do some groundwork, know what to talk about
- ✓ Matchup to the audience at food and drinks
- ✓ Express your gratitude

Things to talk while having lunch or dinner with your boss:

- ✓ Sports
- ✓ Music
- ✓ Literature: depending on his/her age
- ✓ Office history: their years of experience, his/her climb up, his/her challenges
- ✓ Assignments/ Projects
- ✓ Food
- ✓ Hobbies

Few things which your boss may want to hear from you

- ✓ Things you enjoy doing
- ✓ Things you find boring
- ✓ About your knowledge gaps
- ✓ Feedback and goals
- ✓ New innovative methods to implement
- ✓ How your life has been influenced by the company
- ✓ Career progression

Things to avoid talking while having lunch with your boss:

- ✓ Don't get too personal:
- ✓ Strictly avoid prejudiced topics
- ✓ Do not blabber/ blurt out others mistakes
- ✓ Be careful about your remarks: Think of the repercussions before you speak
- ✓ Do not whine or complain
- ✓ Never talk office politics/ gossip
- ✓ Toilet humor
- ✓ Indiscretions: You cross your limit and lose the impression in front of the boss

Staying in Touch- Maintaining and Building your Network

- ✓ Maintaining your existing network is just as important, if not more so, than growing it. If you haven't been in touch with some of your contacts recently, send them a brief email or arrange a meeting to catch up? Nurturing these relationships will help to ensure they remain effective and beneficial over time. If you send an email or leave a message for someone and it isn't urgent, give them a few days to respond before trying them again. Remember that people are busy and may not always have a chance to come back to you immediately.
- ✓ Become active in professional associations and organizations. In order to maintain your network of contacts, you must stay in touch with them. One easy way to stay in touch with your existing contacts and make new contacts is by being active in your professional association and/or in groups in your respective domain. Being active in your professional bodies will keep you in regular contact with your professional peers and will give you an opportunity outside of your job to make new contacts in your field. Being active in civic organizations, non-profit associations, church or other groups provides you the opportunity to connect with others who share your personal interests and values apart from your job. These types of contacts can also be

extremely valuable to you as you manage your career/business over time, while considering a career change or are seeking an alternative opinion or point of view on a challenge you are facing.

- ✓ Maintain a professional presence online (not just a social one!). Professional networking sites like LinkedIn are growing at a very fast rate. Unlike other social media sites, these sites are intended specifically for professional/business networking- they offer professionals with similar interests, backgrounds and skills to connect online and exchange information, recommend peers, make referrals, discuss topics of professional interest, share job leads and offer/seek advice. Professional networking sites are a great complement to the personal networking necessary for a successful job search or even business opportunities. Keep updating your profile regularly.
- ✓ It is important to add value to your network, as well as derive value from it. If someone asks you for help, advice or guidance, try to assist them if you can, or put them in touch with someone else who can help. You might also be able to offer your knowledge and expertise by contributing to relevant discussions on professional networking sites, such as LinkedIn. Depending on your contacts and their needs, you might also be able to introduce people to one another, or share relevant articles or pieces of research/valuable information with them. Help others when they ask for your assistance or advice. Do unto

others as you would have them do unto you! Remember- genuine networking is about reciprocity. When someone genuinely asks for your assistance and you believe you can help, offer your assistance. When you don't believe you can help, let them know. Don't leave them hanging. You wouldn't want them to do that to you.

- ✓ Make a difference. How are you making a difference in the world; in your workplace, in your home, in your community; in the lives of your subordinates, friends and colleagues? Are you making a difference? We all search for meaning, and each person has a different definition of what holds meaning (of what is important) to them. Why do you do what you do? What advice do you have to share with others facing decisions you have had to make in the past? What might you do next? How are you going to get there? You have just as many answers as you have questions. Your answers and advice could really make a difference in someone's career, just as the answers and advice you get will make a difference in yours.
- ✓ Share your expertise. If you are already a strong networker, you will have a lot of skills and expertise that some of your less experienced colleagues might be able to benefit from. If you know someone who is struggling with networking, why not offer to provide them with some advice, or even informal coaching? If you are interested in sharing your expertise on a larger scale, you could offer to facilitate a training session on

networking for the rest of your team or organization.

- ✓ We remember 10% of what we read, 20% of what we hear, 30% of what we see, 50% of what we see and hear, 70% of what we discuss with others, 80% of what we personally experience and 95% of what we teach others. So teaching others can actually help you immensely.

International Networking Etiquette

Etiquette is heavily influenced by culture; each country and nation having their own set of rules for polite behaviour. The world has more than 200 countries, with many containing multiple cultures. When dealing with an international clientele, or when conducting business in a foreign country, it's best to be aware of local etiquette guidelines. Knowing the proper business etiquette for the country of your potential client or partner is the key to success of your business transaction. By following respected and time honoured business etiquette traditions, you will effectively demonstrate your own intellect and class, proving to your foreign business partners that you are worthy and deserving of their attention, respect and business.

Research and Preparation is Paramount: Preparation is the key to ensuring a positive impact: What may be good manners in one country or to one nation may not be good manners in another. Always take the time to research cross-cultural etiquette when dealing with a foreign client, or when conducting business in a foreign country. Awareness of international etiquette is important not just in face-to-face meetings but also in non face-to-face encounters such as sending gifts, conversing over the phone or communicating online. Areas you need to look at include: Religion, Dress code- what attire is appropriate, Social hierarchy, Use of titles and forms of address, Business card /Handshake exchange, Non-verbal communication -what is read between the lines, Introductions-how to get started on the right foot, Personal interactions- Topics to be discussed and not discussed, Valuing Time, Physical Space, Dealing with embarrassment, Gift exchange, How to work with an interpreter

General Tips

Here are some important points when dealing with other cultures:

- ✓ Some cultures dress conservatively as the norm. Americans tend to be more relaxed when it comes to dress codes, and even recommend dressing for comfort in certain fields and professions. People from other parts of the world are generally more conservative. The Japanese, for example, dress according to rank. Some Muslim nations find short dresses for women as offensive. If uncertain, stick to the safer side of conservatism.
- ✓ Some cultures meet and greet people with a kiss, a hug, or a bow instead of a handshake. A handshake for greeting is mostly universal. However, don't be surprised if you are occasionally met with a kiss, a hug, or a bow somewhere along the way.
- ✓ Stick to formal titles for business interactions unless invited otherwise. Approach first names with caution when dealing with people from other cultures. Some cultures are very hierarchical, and will consider it disrespect to be addressed without their title. Some cultures never accept first names in the business setting, and this should be respected.
- ✓ Some cultures are less time-conscious than others. Don't take it personally if someone from a more relaxed culture keeps you waiting or spends more time than you normally would

in meetings or over meals. Stick to the rules of punctuality, but be understanding when your contact from another country seems unconcerned.

- ✓ Understand differences in perception of personal space. Americans have a particular value for their own physical space and are uncomfortable when other people get in their realm. If the international visitor seems to want to be close, accept it. Backing away can send the wrong message
- ✓ Making eye contact: Don't be alarmed when a guest from France or Middle East locks eyes with you and gives a prolonged intense stare. This is common, in fact, the guest may move even closer to get better eye contact. The opposite is true with Britons. Each country will be slightly different in their non-verbal communication and the amount of personal space that they leave. Don't assume it is OK to touch someone.
- ✓ Business Cards: The degree of formality of business card etiquette varies from country to country. In general present your business card with both hands holding the top corners so recipient can read it. Also receive business cards with both hands when possible. It is considered respectful to spend time reading their card. Asians assume you will have a business card holder, so putting a card in your pocket is considered crude. Many nationalities like to have their language printed on the back to help translate the title (South America, Asia, and Northern Europe). Do not write on their business card, as this is defacing the card

- ✓ Body Language: Not only do other cultures speak a foreign language, the body language and gestures are different too. Showing the soles of your shoes while crossing your legs is very offensive with many other cultures. A finger on the nose means "confidentially" to a Briton. Nodding the head means "no" instead of "yes" in Greece and Turkey. Thumbs up is an offensive gesture in parts of Latin America and Africa
- ✓ Accepting a drink: Alcohol is common in many of the international cultures, so be prepared to be offered a drink. Do not turn down an offer of vodka from a business associate from Russia as this is considered highly offensive
- ✓ Gifts: Gifts are given to show gratitude, including as a way to thank someone for a hospitable act. If you are the host, it is not always appropriate to give a gift. Choosing the right gift and presentation is important - wrap the gift, using red or yellow paper - avoid white or black wrappers and ribbons

  Give at the end of meeting, presenting and receiving with both hands but expect polite refusal at first. Other considerations: With Chinese, the gift must be given in a group setting or it will appear to be a bribe. With Japan, the gift should be wrapped or it may be considered rude- It's all about the box. Other cultures place meaning on symbols, colors and number. For example, a clock may be considered a death gift in China. The number 4 is extremely unlucky and will be taken with offense in certain places. Do not open the gift unless you are invited to. Present your gift at the end of the meeting or agreed upon time. Be aware of the culture you are in when wrapping the gift. Always carry three levels of gifts to use as appropriate

- ✓ Topics to avoid: Jokes as some may not understand and they usually don't translate. Negative comments about guests' country's policies or policy makers, and religion, etc must be avoided

Here are some tips by specific country:

South East Asia

China

Being on time is vital

Use formal titles when introducing yourself. Have your business cards printed in Chinese and present business cards with both hands. Exchange business cards at the beginning of the meeting during the introductions. Include gold embossing on your card because it represents wealth, status, and prestige in Chinese cultures. Upon receiving your colleagues' business cards, read them attentively before putting them away carefully and respectfully. Putting a business card directly into your pocket without reading it is highly insulting to Chinese businesspeople. The way you treat the business cards indicates the degree to which you value your relationship with them.

Introduce and address your Chinese colleagues by title and last name, never by first name. During introductions, avoid overly strong handshakes because they are considered offensive and inappropriate for business meetings. Following the introductions, start with small talk before moving on to more serious business matters.

Avoid direct eye contact. Do not offer gifts privately, as these are considered forms of bribery. Do not physically touch your Chinese colleagues.

Where possible, suggest "I'll look into," rather than the closed option of "No."

Wear conservative, dark, simple attire. Bright colors and/or ornate designs are considered flashy and inappropriate. Use conservative suits with subtle colors; Women should avoid high heels and revealing clothing

Do not only discuss business at meals. Speak slowly and pause between your sentences when speaking during a business meeting. At the table try every dish offered

The Chinese hosts should leave the meal first

Japan

Japan has the second largest economy in the world with about 130 million people that speak Japanese world-wide making it the ninth most common language- also the third largest group of internet users.

Avoid using harsh language, refrain from being confrontational and from openly disagreeing with your Japanese colleagues. The Japanese value trustworthy business partners.

Be prepared to answer direct questions such as “How much money do you make?” or “How old are you?” These questions are not considered offensive in Japan and are a way for your Japanese colleagues getting to know you

The customary greeting is a bow. It is proper to exchange business cards at the beginning of the meeting and be sure to take time to read your colleagues’ cards before putting it away carefully and respectfully. It is customary to bow slightly when handing out your card. When toasting, do not lift your glass off the table. Respect personal space. Silence is valued in Japan, so do not force conversation at dinner. Do not be surprised if your Japanese colleagues go silent and close their eyes. This is a sign they are thinking critically.

Dress indicates status; dress to impress. Men should wear dark, conservative suits. Women should not wear pants and should wear low shoes. Do not slurp your noodles to indicate you have enjoyed them. It is appropriate for women to drink at dinner if the host orders drinks for the group

Korea

Present your business card with both hands, and, as with Chinese or Japanese associates, be sure to attentively read your Korean colleague's card before putting it away. Acknowledge those with highest status first, followed by the oldest.

Wear a dark-colored conservative business suit to meetings. When in a Korean business meeting, instead of directly saying "no", show your disagreement by inhaling through closed teeth, tipping back your head, and saying "maybe". When speaking to your Korean associates be sure to pause frequently to allow for questions and deliberations.

Send proposals and meeting agendas prior to the meeting to allow your Korean colleagues some time to review them. Expect your Korean colleagues to deliberate with each other before making a decision.

Some of the values respected in Korea are: Certainty and structure, Collectivity and Team Work, Conformity, Loyalty, Obedience and respect for authority

Europe

UK

Attire should be conservative- Men should wear laced shoes preferably, formal.

Avoid personal questions or staring. Eye contact is rarely maintained throughout a conversation. Respect personal space. Business lunches are often conducted in a pub.

Do not discuss work at after-hours social events. Do not toast anyone older than you

France

Businessmen and women in French-speaking countries value formality and respect in a business relationship. Dress conservatively. Exchange of business cards is most often after initial introductions. Maintain eye contact during discussions. Exaggeration is interpreted as boasting, and even rude. Do not be afraid to debate with your French colleagues. Business partners who make logical arguments and have well rounded views are valued by the French. Avoid overly friendly behavior. Do not discuss business during meals.

Germany

German is one of the most widely spoken languages in Europe and two-thirds of all international trade fairs take place in Germany. Keep in mind that German business etiquette is strict and distinct from most other European countries.

Until you are personally invited to use a colleague's first name, address him or her by surname and title. Punctuality is paramount in a German business meeting so at all costs, avoid being late. Dress conservatively with minimal accessories. Maintain eye contact when speaking and listening. Shake hands before and after a business meeting with a firm, brief handshake to everyone in the room. Formally write up decisions and meeting notes and share them with your German colleagues.

Always knock before entering a room and allow those in higher positions to enter first. When a man and woman are of equal status, the man will enter first. Also, wait to sit until being instructed. The most senior-ranking individual will most often direct you.

Avoid extending meetings past their established schedules. Avoid exaggeration and high pressure talk.

Italy

When scheduling meetings, do it well in advance, with the most appropriate manner being in writing and reconfirming the same with a call. Business meetings are a time for each party to discuss ideas and issues, but not to make decisions, so avoid high-pressure tactics and do not expect decisions to be made. Expect your Italian colleagues to be descriptive, talkative and demonstrative. Italians value personal relationships, so third-party introductions are helpful.

Wear a few elegant accessories, as this display of wealth translates to power in the business arena. It is also very important to honor all agreed-upon verbal commitments in order to maintain credibility with your Italian business colleagues. In addition to a business card, it is important to have a social card, containing name, phone number, title, and academic degree, for non-business interactions.

Spain

Spanish businessmen will prefer to do business with people they know, so they may want to get to know you better through dinner or other social engagements before a business meeting takes place. Wear conservative business suits with a few accessories to indicate status and wealth, and to increase credibility. Communicate face-to-face whenever possible.

It is important to accept their invitations to prove your willingness to do business. Also, it is preferable that you be introduced to prospective Spanish clients through a mutual acquaintance. Once a business meeting is scheduled, do not be surprised if your Spanish associates arrive 15 minutes late. As always, you should arrive on time despite your colleagues' expected lateness. During meetings, expect Spanish colleagues to stray from the agenda.

Once a personal relationship is established, your Spanish colleagues will be loyal to you, not to the company you work for. Expect your Spanish colleagues to deliberate after a meeting rather than make a decision in your presence during the meeting.

Establish an oral agreement before drawing up a formal contract

Russia

Shake hands firmly and maintain eye contact while doing business with Russians. Wear dark, conservative business suits. Women should wear knee length skirts rather than pants-suit. Russians value patience and appreciate the opportunity to debate and digest negotiations. Avoid pressuring your Russian colleagues into making decisions, as this is considered rude and unprofessional.

While your Russian associates may not be on time for meetings, they expect that foreign counterparts will be punctual, if not early. Also, do not expect an apology from a tardy Russian colleague as they consider their behavior a test of your patience.

If discussing technical issues during your meeting, bring an expert along with you. Russians expect a thorough presentation and want to fully understand the topic before making a decision. Expect Russians to display emotion by becoming angry, storming out of meetings, or threatening to terminate your business in an attempt to gain the upper hand in negotiations.

Avoid showing the soles of shoes as this is considered highly disrespectful.

Middle East-Arabic Business Etiquette

Rather than greeting with a "hello" or "good morning," greet your Arab associate with the traditional Islamic greeting "Assalamo Alaikum," which translates to "May peace be upon you and may God's blessings be with you."

When planning a meeting, keep in mind Islamic principles and culture value structure. When choosing a restaurant, respect Islamic dietary restrictions. Some of your Islamic associates may not eat meat or pork so be sure there is an abundance of vegetarian options. Refrain from smoking cigarettes, drinking alcohol and consuming caffeine during meetings.

Certain values like consistency, loyalty, and respect for authority are very much respected in Arab countries. By creating and staying with a set agenda, you will demonstrate not only your organization and business savvy, but also your knowledge of and respect for Arabic business etiquette.

Bahrain: Smiling and direct eye contacts are essential parts of proper business etiquette in

Bahrain. Don't be surprised if your Bahrain partner gives and expects a kiss on the cheek upon greeting you!

Saudi Arabia: Outsiders are subject to Saudi Islamic law, which bans alcohol, drugs, pornography and pork.

United Arab Emirates: The lobbies of large hotels are the preferred venue for business meetings in the UAE, as these rooms limit distraction and give attendants easy access to refreshments.

Follow-up: Thank you notes

The Thank You Note

When to send one: A handwritten thank you note must be sent in response to:

- ✓ A Meeting after en event/ conference
- ✓ Gifts- any kind
- ✓ Dinner, parties or get-togethers
- ✓ After a meal outside/ or at their home
- ✓ Congratulations- on a milestone, an event or achievement, job/college interview
- ✓ Contributions made- sponsors of any of your events, fund raiser, etc.
- ✓ Any other time that is appropriate

Remember that it takes only a minute to write a quick note, but the reward is much greater than just a verbal "thank you" or phone call. A thank you note need not be lengthy- its purpose is only to convey gratefulness. Your note should be sent in a timely manner, however better late than never

What should Thank You Notes cover?

A note has two advantages: a) it doesn't interrupt the other person's time 2) it comes across as warmer and more gracious. This is why it is more preferred to a phone call.

It must ideally contain:

- ✓ A formal greeting and salutation
- ✓ A display of gratitude-Something unique, special or memorable about the event, gift or gesture

- ✓ Expressing to the guest how nice it was to dine with him/ her and briefly recapping any business details.
- ✓ Any details that show that you remember the party/ event and how you had a good time

How should the notes be?

- ✓ Notes should be sent promptly.
- ✓ Thank you notes are usually written on a small fold-over note (usually 3 x 5 or 4 x 6) or on a correspondence card (flat card, usually 4 x 6)
- ✓ If using the fold-over note, write on page 3. If using the correspondence card, write only on the front. Use Blue or Black Ink
- ✓ Begin with the Greeting: *Dear Aubrey,* Write your appreciation: *The Gold Fountain Pen you sent me is just amazing. It looks so elegant in my pocket-Appreciate a lot and thank you very much!* Mention its use: *I am sure going to use this every day, while in the office and even as I move around.* Look ahead: *I'm looking forward to seeing you soon during the next meeting the association has in September. Close: Kind Regards, Carlton*

Here's a sample:

Dear Sarah,

Thank you for that delicious dinner we had last night. I really appreciate all the trouble you put in, in going out of the way to make Jonathan and myself so at ease.

Most of all were those helpful and powerful inputs that you shared with us that will now enable us have a clearer understanding of the upcoming project that we are so excited to be working along with you. I

know together, we will make this a resounding success!
Thank you once again.

Sincerely yours,
Gerard
Title
Company Name (logo)

Reciprocating to the Invitation

When you invite someone to a business lunch, dinner, or breakfast, it does not always mean they are obligated to reciprocate. This is particularly more appropriate to business situations where you are not expected to repay an invitation to a strictly-business meal, no matter who invited you - a customer, a client, or your boss. But you may certainly want to do so if you are looking at continuing business together. So also, it applies to a customer who has been entertained by a salesperson or supplier-is not expected to return the invitation, even if his or her spouse or family was invited.

However, for social settings, you will need to return social invitations from your colleagues, friends and other business associates.

Conclusion

Success may look different for everyone, but practicing good networking skills, being professional, productive and respectful to people around you will help you achieve your ultimate goal. These skills will not only serve you well now, but also in the future. In today's competitive environment, carrying yourself professionally and managing yourself at various opportunities is an area of expertise that is much sought after.

Remember the old adage that *"no (hu)man is an island"?* Well, it turns out that the saying holds a lot of truth. There's no denying that anyone that is doing outstandingly well has not achieved it, only on their own. Instead, their success in large part is thanks to the wider network that they nurtured and leveraged as they took each step to greater heights.

Therefore, Networking is a two-way street- it can take you to where you want to go, but you have to put your car in gear, follow the traffic laws, and show courtesy to your fellow drivers on the networking highway. It will also help to use a GPS or map, because if you don't know where you're going, you'll never know when you get there. So move ahead and hit the road and start networking!

As with leadership, I believe that networking skills are very important. And what's even more important, however, is working to improve them and learning how to use them effectively. That's what really counts.

Finally, when you become comfortable with what you've learned, most of this becomes second nature-

completely natural to you. Remember, that knowing most of this information and being sincere, will give you the confidence to tackle all situations ahead of you, so you can concentrate on developing your business at hand!
And if you do forget some of this, you have one very important rule to remember and fall back on- Always use: Common sense, Respect, Compassion, Sincerity and Kindness. Always take the higher ground, and do not respond to rudeness with rudeness.

Remember networking is about building lasting connections, so slow and steady will win this race!

About the Author
'GERARD ASSEY'

Gerard Assey is a Graduate in Economics, a PGD in Management (HRD) and holds a Doctorate in Leadership. Gerard holds several International Qualifications in Sales, Debt Collection, Training & Teaching, and is a 'Fellow' of the prestigious 'Institute of Sales & Marketing Management'-UK, a Certified NLP Practitioner, a 'Certified Trainer', an 'Accredited Management Teacher-Behavioral Sciences', a 'Certified Competency Facilitator', a 'Certified Management Consultant'- (the International credentials of a professional management consultant, awarded in accordance with global standards of the ICMCI); and a Certification from the University of Michigan in 'Successful Negotiation: Essential Strategies and Skills'

He is also a Member of the 'National Association of Sales Professionals' backed with several years experience in varied industries, both in India and Overseas. He also holds an 'Etiquette Consultant' Certification from the USA (by Sue Fox, Author of Best Seller: 'Business Etiquette for Dummies'. She has trained some of the top celebrities' world over). He was also a recipient of a scholarship for extensive training in Japan on 'Corporate Management for India'.

Gerard Assey is 'Founder & Chief Corporate Trainer' of the Group: '**Citius, Altius, Fortius Unlimited**'- an organization that **celebrated 20 years of Glorious Service** in 2021, focusing on 3 Core Competencies:

People. Performance. Profit; in functional areas of Sales & Marketing, HR & Organizational Development, covering Recruitment, Training & Consultancy!

Having managed organizations with large Sales Forces in India & Overseas, his specialization cover extensive areas of Sales Training (All levels - Presentation, Negotiation, Key/ Strategic Accounts Management & Managerial Skills for all sectors), Bid Proposal/ Capture Planning/ Management Trainings, Retail Sales, Customer Service & Customer Retention Programs, Training for Prevention & Collection of Debt, Self & Personal Development Programs (Time Management, Teamwork & Team Building, Business Etiquette & Personal Grooming, Leadership & Managerial Skills, People Management Skills, Train-the-Trainer etc), including preparation of Custom-designed Business Manuals for Internal (HR, Induction, and Sales etc) & External use (Instruction, User Manuals).

Gerard has successfully conducted over 5900 Trainings & Workshops (as of Nov '22) all across India, Middle East, Africa, Europe & S.E. Asia. Besides public programs conducted regularly, both in India & Overseas, he has some of the top names as clients whom he services from Single Owners to large Public & Government undertakings, covering all sectors, for their in-house needs.

His website: www.CollectionSkills.com is the only one in this part of the world to be featured in the 'Collections & Credit Risk Magazine-USA' under 'Who's Who in Training' and ranks TOP, along with other websites listed below on most search engines.

Gerard is author of 49 books already (as on Nov 2022),

A few of the business related books being:

1. Bite-sized Bits on Commonsense Management
2. Heart to Heart on Life's Principles'
3. How to become a Successful Manager
4. The Sales Professionals' Master Workbook of S.Y.S.T.E.M.S
5. The Professional Business Email Etiquette Handbook & Guide
6. The Professional Business Video-Conferencing Etiquette Handbook & Guide
7. Professional Presentation Skills
8. Exceptional Customer Service
9. Professional Tele-Marketing Skills
10. Professional Debt Collection Skills
11. The G.R.E.A.T. Sales & Service Workbook
12. Sales Training Advantage for Results (*The Ultimate Sales Training Manual*
    to enable you stand out as a S.T.A.R.)
13. CEO Daily Planner & Organizer
14. The Sales Professionals' Master Daily Planner
15. The Professional Debt Collector's Master Daily Planner
16. My Daily Planner & Organizer
17. MY EMERGENCY INFORMATION RECORD (Family Emergency & Peace of Mind Planner)
18. The Ultimate Therapist & Counselors Planner and Organizer
19. Building an Ethical Workplace
20. Managing Relationships at Work
21. Managing Business Meetings Effectively
22. Effective Delegation Skills
23. Goal Setting for Success
24. B2B Selling by Email
25. Professional Business Etiquette & Grooming
26. Dining Etiquette & Table Manners
27. Effective Networking Skills

Besides regularly contributing to business & trade journals, including international ones such as the 'Creative Training Techniques' and the 'Sales News' of the U.S.A, He is also a member of several prestigious bodies & trade associations, having participated in many Conferences & Workshops in India & Overseas.

Prior to his last assignment of leading & managing a large MNC as head, Gerard had a 3-year stint in the Middle East as a Consultant with a leading British Consultancy Firm.

As the past 'Official Country Representative' for the International Business Award- 'THE STEVIES'-(the business world's own Oscar) for about 4 years- he ensured a few Indian companies that qualify for the same every year!

Gerard can be contacted at:

Email: training@Sales-Training.in,training@CollectionSkills.com
Websites:

www.Sales-Training.in
www.EtiquetteWorks.in
www.CollectionSkills.com
www.RetailSalesTraining.in
www.SalesTrainingIndia.com
www.ManualPreparation.com
www.TrainingWithPuppets.com
www.FirstContactAcademy.com
www.SalesAndMarketingRecruiter.com

Our TRAININGS & BOOKS that can help your team

- ✓ **Sales Effectiveness**: Selling Skills for any Sector: Service/ Logistics/ FMCG Realty/ Insurance & Finance/ Media/ SPA's, Health Clubs & Salons/ Key Account Management, Effective Negotiation Skills/ Bid & Proposal Management Skills/ Retail Sales Training: Any Sector (Auto, Jewelry, Clothing, Luxury etc)
- ✓ **Customer Service Skills**-Complaints Handling & Customer Retention
- ✓ **Debt Prevention & Collection Skills**
- ✓ **Etiquette & Grooming**
- ✓ **Leadership & Managerial Skills**
- ✓ **Self & Personal Development Skills**: Presentation Skills/ Effective Communication Skills/Business Proposal Writing Skills/ Problem Solving & Decision Making Skills/ Empowering Secretaries-The perfect PA! (For Secretaries & PA's)/ Effective Time Management/ Teamwork & Teambuilding/ P.R.I.D.E- **P**ersonal **R**esponsibility **I**n **D**elivering **E**xcellence

www.ingramcontent.com/pod-product-compliance
Lightning Source LLC
LaVergne TN
LVHW010110170826
845678LV00012B/2336

* 9 7 8 9 3 9 2 4 9 2 3 6 5 *